Advance Praise for *Heroism and Hope*

"In *Heroism and Hope*, Dr. David Bryfman zeroes in on a key factor that shapes our comprehension and worldview like no other: education. Bryfman's wealth of experience in the field of Jewish and Israel education has generated an indispensable tool or understanding the reverberations of the October 7 rupture throughout the Jewish world. I am confident this book will enrich the important conversations beginning to take place since, concerning the scope and particularly the focus of Israel education, and I am sincerely encouraged by the vision its author presents."

—President, State of Israel, Isaac Herzog

"David Bryfman has long been one of the most thoughtful, bold, and creative thinkers in the field of Israel education. In *Heroism and Hope*, he brings that insight to one of the defining challenges facing the Jewish community today: how to educate a new generation of Jews about Israel in the aftermath of October 7. With intellectual honesty and deep educational wisdom, Bryfman challenges educators to move beyond slogans and reactive advocacy toward a richer, more meaningful approach, one that embraces complexity, strengthens Jewish identity, and fosters genuine connection to Israel and the Jewish people. At a moment of uncertainty and searching, this book offers both clarity and hope. It is an important and timely contribution to the evolving field of Israel education."

—Rabbi B. Elka Abrahamson,
president, The Wexner Foundation

"Bryfman has written the definitive manifesto for Israel education in this new era. He understands that Israel is central to the development of Jewish identity, and this book will ensure that educators at every level also see this truth. As too many today are playing whack-a-mole, dealing with the latest antisemitic incident of the moment, Bryfman counsels us to play the long game. He understands that to make sure our next generation cares about Jewish Peoplehood, they must have pride—including pride in Israel—which comes from a combination of deep Jewish knowledge and intimate personal connection. Bryfman offers us the recipe; now it's up to our educators to cook up this new batch of chicken soup for the Jewish soul."

—Zack Bodner, president and
CEO, Oshman Family JCC

"In a world dominated by binaries, generational divides, and hardening hearts, the need for Israel education that is both substantive and textured has never been more acute. Dr. David Bryfman, the preeminent Israel educator of our age, has provided us with an inspired and inspiring vade mecum for navigating our uncharted terrain. Anyone invested in the future of Jewish and Israel education would do well to read it, teach from it, and return to it often."

—Rabbi Dr. Elliot Cosgrove, Park Avenue Synagogue

"In *Heroism and Hope*, David Bryfman offers not slogans but soul-work, reminding us that loving Israel means teaching it truthfully, bravely, and with deep faith in our learners' capacity for nuance and empathy. This is essential reading for anyone committed to raising a Jewish generation rooted in integrity, peoplehood, and hope."

—Rabbi Menachem Creditor, scholar-in-residence, UJA-Federation of New York

"Across global Jewish education—from day schools to summer camps—educators everywhere have felt the ground shift beneath their feet since October 7. Bryfman's *Heroism and Hope* speaks to all of them, across denominations and geographies, with a shared language of purpose, resilience, and love for the Jewish people. With intellectual honesty and incisive clarity, the book diagnoses the challenges of contemporary Israel education and proposes a bold reconceptualization rooted in Jewish thought and modern pedagogy."

—Dr. Howard Deitcher, Melton Centre for Jewish Education at the Hebrew University

"David Bryfman has given us a powerful manifesto and call to action to reimagine Israel education for a post–October 7 world. At once personal and philosophical and practical, this book is an essential guide to reshaping Israel education for a new generation of educators and learners. David is one of the most insightful thinkers on Jewish and Israel education today, and he offers a visionary and proactive framework for educators and stakeholders in the field, as well as tangible ideas for the changes needed to ensure Israel education is relevant and integral to forging strong Jewish identity, peoplehood, and commitment to Israel for the future. At a pivotal turning point for the Jewish people and Israel, *Heroism and Hope* is an important contribution to our community and our canon."

—Lisa Eisen, co-president, Charles and Lynn Schusterman Family Philanthropies

"In a moment defined by shock, division, and exhaustion, *Heroism and Hope* offers something rare: a path forward grounded in trust in educators and faith in learners. David Bryfman brings wisdom, honesty, and heart to the hardest questions facing Israel education after October 7. This book reminds us that good education does not shield young people from complexity—it prepares them to meet it with courage."

—Barry Finestone, president and CEO, Jim Joseph Foundation

"In the wake of October 7 and its aftermath, urgent questions have emerged about the past, present, and future of Jewish and Israel education. In *Heroism and Hope*, Dr. David Bryfman confronts these questions with clarity, honesty, and deep care for the field he has helped shape. Bryfman challenges educators to engage Israel and the Jewish community as they truly are—layered, complex, and often uncomfortable. Bryfman reminds us that Israel education cannot be reduced to advocacy, messaging, or certainty. With intellectual rigor and moral seriousness, he invites us to rethink the relationship between educator and learner, to expand the frameworks through which we teach about Israel, and to embrace the reality that meaningful Israel education must hold complexity rather than avoid it. In doing so, he reminds us that grappling with difficult questions is not a threat to connection with Israel; it is the very foundation of an authentic and enduring one. Written with both urgency and hope, this book calls on educators, communal leaders, and learners alike to lean into diversity of thought, deepen their understanding, and recommit to the educational work that lies ahead. *Heroism and Hope* is essential reading for anyone seeking to understand where Israel education stands today—and to imagine where it must go next."

—Dr. Keren E. Fraiman, vice president
and chief academic officer, Spertus Institute
for Jewish Learning and Leadership

"October 7 and its aftermath has forced a deep reset for the entire field of Israel education. David Bryfman, one of the most trusted educators in Jewish life, has written an important new book, *Heroism and Hope*, which is a guidebook we all need. Probing, agitational, balanced, and wise without the false certainty of an idealogue, his book will help educators successfully navigate the daunting new minefield that is Israel education into a more promising future."

—Rabbi Rick Jacobs, president,
Union for Reform Judaism

"In a world shaken by October 7, David Bryfman offers something Jewish education urgently needed: intellectual courage and genuine hope. *Heroism and Hope* does not avoid different opinions; it embraces them—and reminds us that educating about Israel is not about defending positions, but about enabling people capable of thinking, feeling, and engaging deeply. The type of Zionism which inspires me is the one expressed in the Declaration of Independence: one that calls for diversity, honors the dignity of every person, and perceives democracy as a value, not merely as a system. Bryfman writes with that same spirit. This book is a compass for educators who, amid the background noise, still believe that the Jewish people can unite around what makes us greater, not what divides us."

—Silvio Joskowicz, chairman of the Department
of Zionist Enterprises, World Zionist Organization

"As David's Israeli colleague (and hopefully friend), we've been working in the Israel education field together for many years—navigating some of the most complex challenges we've ever known in the past two and a half years. What I appreciate about *Heroism and Hope* is the books' vulnerable approach in naming truths many of us are carrying about why Israel education matters, and even more so right now. I see this book as an invitation to put our hearts on the table—and our heads and hands to work in restoring hopeful Israel education."

—Dr. Shelley Kedar, chief impact officer, The Jewish Agency for Israel

"A must read for all who care about Israel and Jewish education. Essential for teachers, executives, foundation and communal leaders who are wrestling with the complex Jewish educational issues in our post–October 7 world."

—Dr. John Ruskay, executive vice president emeritus, UJA-Federation of New York

"This work demonstrates most clearly why David Bryfman is thought of as the Dean of Jewish and Israel Education of North America. His capacity to turn the tough questions of post–October 7 Jewish life into educator lessons is both profound and uplifting. Not since Jonathan Woocher's *Sacred Survival* has there been a work that so speaks to this moment in diaspora Jewish life. It needs to be read by stakeholders well beyond educators. All those with an investment in the future of the Jewish community would benefit from its lessons."

—Dr. Jeffrey R. Solomon, president emeritus, Andrea and Charles Bronfman Philanthropies

"David has presented a challenging—even controversial in parts—picture of the changing face of diaspora Jewry's relationship with Israel and their own Jewish identity. Charmingly and effectively, he has done this in parallel to his personal journey from his formative years in Australia, to his current very senior position in Jewish education in the largest diaspora Jewish community in the world. David details the profound effect October 7 had on his own sense of Jewishness and peoplehood, whilst turning this personal and at times questioning thoughtful assessment into a guide for the contemporary Jewish educator. Raising multiple layers of insight and encouraging a more generation-appropriate discussion of dilemmas, rather than providing one-dimensional prescriptive answers that are no longer fit for purpose. A wonderful addition to assist the Jewish educators of today."

—Dr. Ron Weiser, Past President of the Zionist Federation of Australia and Member of the Board of Governors of the Jewish Agency for Israel

"This book is a thoughtful call to recharge Israel education for a new era. David Bryfman pushes educators beyond talking points and toward something deeper: helping learners wrestle with identity, peoplehood, and Israel's place in Jewish life. At a moment when those questions feel especially urgent, this is an important and valuable contribution."

—Dr. Noam L. Weissman, EVP, OpenDor Media

"The trauma of October 7 is all-encompassing but fails to provide us with a vision for the future of Israel education. Bryfman provides that vision by teaching us to focus on Jewish peoplehood, valuing our common destiny as well as our differences, and arguing for a recharged identity infused with knowledge, joy, responsibility, and hope."

—Rabbi Dr. Raphael Zarum, Dean,
London School of Jewish Studies

HEROISM AND HOPE

HEROISM AND HOPE

Recharging Israel Education in a Post–October 7 World

David Bryfman

A WICKED SON BOOK
An Imprint of Post Hill Press
ISBN: 979-8-89565-811-6
ISBN (eBook): 979-8-89565-813-0

Heroism and Hope:
Recharging Israel Education in a Post-October 7 World

Published in partnership with the Z3 Institute. For more information, please visit www.z3project.org.

Cover illustration by Zeev "Shoshke" Engelmayer
Cover design by Aura Lewis

Post Hill Press
New York • Nashville
wickedsonbooks.com
posthillpress.com

Published in the United States of America
1 2 3 4 5 6 7 8 9 10

The day that Eliot and Rebecca told me that
their cousin was one of the hostages and the day
we found out that Hersh was murdered.
The days that Yaffa's and Abby's nephews—both
named Yakir—were IDF soldiers killed in battle.
The day when Dalia—sister-in-law of one freed hostage, Iair,
and one hostage still in captivity, Eitan (since also returned
home alive)—attended my daughter's Bat Mitzvah.
The day Ayala, and then Osnat, and then so many others, told
me that their husbands were being called up to reserve duty
again, each after having already served over three hundred days.

* * *

The whole world reads headlines and scrolls social media.
We Jewish educators have colleagues who are friends,
who are family, who are the Jewish people, and all of us
now hold their names and faces and voices and stories.
This book is written in honor of the victims
of October 7 and its aftermath.
To those who were taken hostage, to the Israeli soldiers
who have given their lives to defend the Jewish people,
to those who have lost their lives under the barrage
of missiles, and to all of the innocent souls in Israel,
in Gaza, and around the world who have lost their
lives and been wounded since that fateful day.
This book is dedicated to the tens of thousands of
Jewish educators around the world, who, despite their
own challenges and struggles, have committed their
lives to bearing witness, creating memory, and ensuring
that we will all dance again and again and again.

TABLE OF CONTENTS

FOREWORD

October 7 has left an indelible mark on Jewish consciousness. In its wake, educators have navigated grief, fear, anger, solidarity, and profound moral questioning—often simultaneously. The instinct to respond swiftly is understandable, as students seek answers, communities seek clarity, leaders seek language, and institutions feel pressure to provide direction.

Yet education—just as identity and communal cohesion—cannot be sustained by urgency alone.

Moments of rupture demand not only response, but reflection as well. If educational work remains confined to reaction, horizons narrow and complexity is reduced. The deeper responsibility of education is not only to address events as they unfold, but to consider what kinds of moral, historical, and civic understanding we seek to cultivate over time.

This volume enters that demanding terrain not as a closed system or a tightly structured treatise under a single conceptual canopy. Rather, it unfolds as the author's personal, and at times deeply intimate journey, engages insights, tensions, challenges, and opportunities in the shadow of crisis. Its pages reflect an educator thinking in motion, wrestling with questions, testing assumptions, and exploring possibilities with seriousness, concern, hope, and intent.

The author, David Bryfman, is a recognized leader in the field of Jewish and Israel education. His institutional leadership and ongoing engagement with educators across diverse contexts provide his work with practical grounding and field awareness. That experience is evident throughout the volume, particularly in its attention to real educational settings and lived institutional realities.

The distinguished educator Barry Chazan has long reminded us that our task is to strive for conceptual clarity while acknowledging the irreducible ambiguity that accompanies any genuine search for understanding. We aim to say what we mean, yet we recognize that meaning unfolds dialogically, historically, and often painfully. Clarity does not eliminate complexity; it dignifies it. Ambiguity does not excuse confusion, but it demands intellectual responsibility, emotional investment, and an empowered sense of humility. Consequently, this foreword should not be read as unqualified endorsement of every argument or formulation within the book. Readers may find areas of strong agreement, areas that invite further development, and areas that stimulate ongoing discussion. Such diversity of response is not a weakness of the work; it is a natural feature of serious engagement with events, ideas, and beliefs unfolding in real time. The purpose here is to position the book within the professional conversation it seeks to advance, not to signal blanket agreement with each of its assumptions or claims.

There is particular value in the book's decision to proceed in a mode of personal exploration rather than formal systematization on behalf of the field. In periods of upheaval, premature conceptual closure can obscure complexity and limit understanding. What is often needed first is disciplined reflection—the willingness to articulate dilemmas clearly, to acknowledge competing commitments, and to consider constructive pathways without overstating certainty. Sure, some proposals offered in this book will resonate immediately; others may spark principled disagreement—but is that not precisely the goal of educational leadership in the first place? It is not argument that we should fear—it is apathy, timidity, conceptual thinness, or moral fatigue that plague these conversations.

The contribution of this volume lies in that engagement. It resists reducing education to messaging and instead attempts to hold together Israel, Jewish peoplehood, responsibility, and moral complexity within a suggested educational frame. It recognizes that removing oneself from zones-of-comfort is essential to meaningful educational work—and that it is a trait we must all learn to master.

No single book can resolve the profound challenges currently facing Jewish and Israel education. In that sense, the book should be read as part of an ongoing educational endeavor, its value rooted not in finality but in advancement: provoking conversation, sharpening reflection, and encouraging thoughtful discourse at a moment when both clarity and humility are required.

For our part, I hope this work is engaged seriously and critically, neither embraced unreflectively nor dismissed reflexively. Our field advances not through unanimity but through principled debate anchored in shared purpose and disciplined thought.

For his genuine effort to trigger such important discourse, David Bryfman deserves our gratitude.

Dr. Zohar Raviv

INTRODUCTION
The Education We Thought We Gave

In the days, weeks, and months following October 7, I began to sense that something had gone very wrong in my chosen field of Jewish and Israel education.

My phone did not stop ringing and my email and WhatsApp did not stop pinging. The calls were not from journalists, politicians, security experts, or lobbyists. They were from parents, grandparents, communal leaders, donors, and educators. Many of them were shaken, angry, and in some cases genuinely disoriented.

Their questions were blunt, sometimes accusatory and sometimes despairing. How did Jewish education fail so badly that Jewish students had ended up pitching tents at Columbia University—and then across the United States and the world—chanting slogans that seemed to place them not just outside the Jewish community but in opposition to it? How had they come to join a political movement that approved of the slaughter of over 1,000 Jews and, in many cases, actively supported those who committed it?

At first, I tried to answer with data. I explained that not all the protesters were students, let alone Jewish. I reminded them the loudest voices were not always the most representative.

None of it mattered. Statistics offered no comfort in the face of what people were witnessing. Ideas that were once on the margins of academic discourse had become normalized in elite institutions and were now infecting the larger society. Those who held them did not criticize Israeli policies but recast Zionism itself as a moral crime and Jewish identity as inherently suspect.

It was not long before a second wave of calls began to arrive. They were angrier, younger, and aimed in the opposite direction.

These callers were often in their twenties and thirties. Some were teenagers. They accused the Jewish community of deception. *You didn't tell us the whole story*, they said. *You lied.* They used a newly weaponized vocabulary—*colonialism*, *apartheid*, *genocide*. These terms had been stripped of their historical and legal definitions and redeployed as moral condemnations. Zionism, once understood as a movement of Jewish self-determination, had been flattened into a slur. Israel was no longer a country but a symbol of everything these callers had been taught to reject.

These voices came from what we lazily call the "right" and the "left," from "Zionists" and "anti-Zionists." They were not fringe. They were not rare. And it was clear that they were not going away.

What united all those who contacted me, beyond shock and fury, was a shared belief that Jewish and Israel education were the root cause of their disillusionment. Parents believed such education had failed to inoculate their children against hatred of Israel and the Jewish community. Young adults believed such education had deceived them.

I knew now that something, whatever it might be, was deeply broken in Jewish and Israel education. I was not certain what it was. But I was certain that it urgently needed to be repaired.

Behind all the criticism, I faced a deeper assumption. Education is something everyone understands, everyone can judge, and everyone feels entitled to redesign.

Education is one of the few professions in which this dynamic is considered normal: despite unprecedented access to information, expertise is often discounted—something we would find absurd in other fields, like patients instructing surgeons based on a past operation or homeowners directing plumbers on major repairs because they once dealt with a clogged drain. The truth is that this somewhat absurd situation came about because education suffers from its own ubiquity. Everyone has been educated, and therefore everyone believes they know how education should work. The result is a field constantly buffeted by outside pressures—political, philanthropic, and ideological—that is rarely allowed to articulate its own standards of excellence.

Nowhere is this more dangerous than in Jewish and Israel education. Perhaps this, I thought, was what had gone wrong.

The Jewish community is currently consumed by debates about red lines and big tents, advocacy strategies and political loyalty, security, fundraising, and public relations. These conversations are understandable andnecessary. But they cannot be the rules by which education operates.

Education is not advocacy. It is not messaging. It is not crisis management. And when it becomes any of those things, it fails. Sometimes it fails quietly, sometimes catastrophically. Good education must be governed by the principles of good education, especially when the stakes feel existential.

In her essay *The Crisis in Education*, written in the aftermath of World War II, Hannah Arendt warned that education is inevitably political because it prepares children to enter a shared world. But she insisted that it must never be partisan. When adults use education to fight their present battles, she argued, they rob children of their future. "Education," she wrote, "is the point at which we decide whether we love the world enough to assume responsibility for it…and whether we love our children enough not to expel them from our world and leave them to their own devices, nor to strike from their hands their chance of undertaking something new, something unforeseen by us, but to prepare them in advance for the task of renewing a common world."[1]

Based on my recent experiences, I believe that Jewish and Israel education must be renewed and rebuilt. But in rebuilding it, we must follow Arendt's advice. Our children deserve better than our panic and our preferred talking points.

Good Israel education cannot be about forcing people to become a particular kind of Jew or an unquestioning lover of Zion, but must instead empower individuals to think critically, wrestle with complexity, and develop their own meaningful relationship with Israel.

We should not rebuild Jewish education because we want better arguments. We should rebuild it because our children deserve an education that is intellectually honest, morally serious, and capable of addressing complexity without collapsing into dogma or despair.

If we want to save the younger generation for the Jewish community, we must establish new parameters for Jewish and Israel education. However, we must not choose those parameters based on whether they make adults more comfortable. We should choose them because they reflect the reality of the twenty-first-century world. This is a world of flattened narratives, algorithmic outrage, moral absolutism, and relentless othering.

We must engage with these issues because, if education does not address them, something else will. And it will likely be something much, much worse.

This book was written in the belief that education can do more than defend our children against toxic rhetoric and ideas. It can replace such toxicity. The vitriol, condemnation, and reflexive tribalism that now define so much adult discourse are not inevitable. Good education can cultivate young Jews who are rooted rather than reactive, critical without being corrosive, proud without being brittle, and connected to Israel without being intellectually coerced.

This is not just about responding to antisemitism or countering misinformation. It is about whether the Jewish people will succeed in raising a new generation of Jews who know who they are, where they come from, and what they stand for. A generation of Jews who can engage with the world without surrendering to it.

Education is not the only tool we have but it may be the most important. We can neither neglect or abuse it. If we are to rebuild Jewish and Israel education, we must always keep this in mind. This is a difficult task, but we are not free to desist from it.

This book is neither a manifesto nor a framework. However, it is also not a passive testament. Instead, it is intended to raise the questions and challenges that confront Jewish educators today and the foreseeable future. This book is about what must be done.

* * *

Over the past year, many people have told me exactly what they want and need Israel education to do, such as to prepare a generation of foot soldiers on college campuses, create more Zionists, or even protest the current Israeli government. Before the release of the remaining living hostages from Gaza, many told me that the only thing that mattered was to apply pressure that would lead to their release.

I empathize with all of these sentiments, so I hate to disappoint, but Israel education is actually about none of those things and, paradoxically, all of those things. Israel education is not about the study of Israel. That is "Israel studies." It is not about developing the knowledge and skills to lobby for or defend Israel. That is "Israel advocacy." Israel education is about the role Israel plays in the lives of Jewish people.

The idea that Israel is an instrument of Jewish identity is not universally accepted. There are many, including Israelis, who resent the use of Israel education for purposes other than learning about Israel. But usually, even Israelis understand that, when we speak about Israel as a tool for enhancing Jewish identity, it is not about manipulation or exploitation. It is about using the very best of Israel to develop a strong relationship between Israel, Israelis, and Jews living around the world.

Understanding that Israel education is about the development of individual identity is critical. It means that Israel education must be considered an integral part of Jewish education. As Dr. Yehuda Kurtzer, President of the Shalom Hartman Institute of North America, has said, "You cannot treat teaching about Israel as some addon or optional module. It has to be central to a Jewish curriculum if you want to cultivate a mature and meaningful Jewish identity."[2]

In the same way that Jewish history, Torah, Talmud, Jewish holidays and values, *tefillah* (prayer), and the Hebrew language all can and should be part of this broader framework, so too should Israel. As we will see throughout this book, educating about Israel can and should foster a positive connection with one's Jewish heritage and identity.

Some will counter that it is possible to be a Jew today without any connection to Israel. But just because some people want to lead a Jewish life without any relationship with Israel does not mean that we as educators should agree. As a Jewish educator, I will continue to teach Jewish atheists about God and prayer, secular Jews about sacred texts, Jews in one community about Jews in other communities, and English speakers the Hebrew language. I believe a relationship with Israel, in any form, is as essential to Jewish education as other components.

However, the aim of this book—and Israel education in general—is not to prescribe an education that suits everyone. All of us are acutely aware of the differences amongst the Jewish people. We know that Jewish education takes place in many settings, formal and informal: in day schools and congregational schools, in summer camps and youth groups, on college campuses and in kindergartens, on Israel trips and online. This book is not designed to be one-size-fits-all. However, it does offer a framework, addresses some of the challenges, and poses many of the questions now before us. These are challenges and questions that all Jewish educators must confront regardless of their differences.

Many readers of this book might anticipate bold measures to empower educators with strategies and tools to combat the challenges of being Jewish in today's world. Certainly, as Jews, we live in uncertain times. Anti-Israel and anti-Jewish vitriol have become commonplace, if not normalized, on campuses, in classrooms, and in public spaces around the globe.

Empowering our youth and young adults to respond to such animosity is crucial. However, reacting to immediate dire circumstances is like playing whack-a-mole, constantly running from one disaster to the next, only to ultimately realize that victory is unattainable. If Jewish and Israel education adopt a defensive stance, they will never be able to address all the challenges faced by our learners.

More important, it will never be able to present a compelling argument for why being a proud Jew with a strong connection to Israel is a worthwhile choice. For Jewish and Israel education to thrive, it must become a proactive force within the Jewish community. It must clearly articulate why a strong relationship with Israel, even in its imperfect state, can and should enhance the meaning of what it is to be a Jew in the contemporary world.

* * *

I am increasingly convinced that, if the Shoah and the establishment of the State of Israel were the defining moments of Jewish civilization in the twentieth century, then October 7 and its aftermath will define what Jewish life will look like in the twenty-first century and beyond.

Even if I am wrong, the past two years have presented realities and challenges to the vast majority of Jewish educators far beyond anything that they have experienced in their lifetimes.

So, in some ways, this book is a marker in time. Its origins lie in the months after October 7. Its epilogue was written in the days after the formal end of the war on the eve of Simchat Torah 2025. But it is more than one educator's reflections. It explains why Jewish education, with Israel as a core component, cannot, should not, and will never be the same following October 7.

The writing of this book began on an El Al flight from Israel on February 1, 2024 after my second trip to Israel since October 7. I have traveled to Israel several more times, with each journey adding additional layers to my relationship with Israel, Israelis, and Israel education.

During my visits, I spoke with hundreds of Israelis. Each person had their own story of where they were on October 7 and were grappling with different struggles and challenges as a result. But the one thing that they all said to me was that Israel has been forever changed.

Following the events of October 7, many Israelis confronted a profound sense of vulnerability that questioned their belief in Israel's invincibility, especially among those who had grown up after the 1973 Yom Kippur War.

This was compounded by widespread distrust of their political leadership, which many felt had permitted the conditions that led the attacks to emerge. Yet there was also a renewed faith in civil society, exemplified by grassroots efforts like the Hostages and Missing Families Forum and widespread community support for the displaced. Israelis also had to navigate the tension between unity and division, as preexisting societal fractures persisted despite slogans of collective resolve. Amid these challenges, trust in the Israel Defense Forces remained steadfast, reflecting the deep connection between the soldiers and their society.

These dynamics revealed a nation grappling with vulnerability, mistrust, division, and hope. There was little doubt in my mind that Israel has indeed fundamentally and irrevocably changed, as the prolonged mourning and the tension between despair and hope became palpable across the country, even though there are already some indications that some aspects of Israeli life might revert to a pre-October 7 state.

If there is even the slightest conjecture as to whether Israel has forever changed since October 7, no one has expressed such debate in regard to the global Jewish community that was also profoundly changed by October 7. Over the past two years, many Jews have experienced a renewed awareness of both their connection to and separateness from Israel. October 7 served as a catalyst for a revival of Jewish engagement, sometimes described as the emergence of the "October 8 Jew," and a surge in Jewish affiliation and activity.

Israelis were deeply moved by the outpouring of solidarity from Jews worldwide and quickly began asking how Jewish life was being affected outside Israel, highlighting a shared sense of responsibility and togetherness, exemplified by efforts to support hostages reminiscent of the Soviet Jewry movement of the 1980s and 1990s.

Jews worldwide have faced increased anti-Israel sentiment, often accompanied by anti-Zionist rhetoric, protests, and even violence, particularly among younger generations in online spaces. These challenges have compelled Jews to balance acceptance with hatred, belonging with isolation, and pride with disillusionment, transforming Jewish life globally and highlighting both the fragility and resilience of the Jewish people over the past two years.

* * *

Of course, my assessment that Israel and the Jewish world are forever changed could be wrong. The spirit of Israeli resilience and revival, along with Jewish steadfastness and pride might bring things "back to normal" in a short time.

However, I am certain that I am not wrong regarding the need for Israel education to change as a response to October 7. I will go as far as to say that the changes necessary will be some of the greatest since 1967, 1973, and even 1948. But unlike many of the changes experienced by Israel and the Jewish people since October 7, the Jewish community and all of its educators and stakeholders have agency over these changes. We can bring about the changes that are necessary. We must convince people of the need for change.

As an educator, I am attuned to listening to people's stories while being empathetic and non-judgmental. When they tell me that their realities are forever changed, I choose to believe them. Jewish educators from around the world are telling me that, because of many of the tensions outlined above, the conditions under which they are operating and the learners and families they serve are completely different today. They need and even demand a new vision and pedagogy for Israel education in a post-October 7 world. For this reason alone, it is clear that Israel education must change.

However, this book is not a critique of Jewish educators. It is an attempt to recharge Jewish educators who are exhausted in a post-Covid and post-October 7 world, and to offer them a clear path forward. A call to reimagine Israel education could not be made without faith in the people who must implement this change. Moreover, I do not dismiss the decades of work that have been done to establish Israel education as a significant force in Jewish learning.

I think instead of Berl Katznelson, a central figure in the Labor Zionist movement, for whom Kibbutz Be'eri, one of the kibbutzim hardest hit on October 7, was named. He wrote:

> A renewing and creative generation does not throw the cultural heritage of ages into the dustbin. It examines and scrutinizes, accepts and rejects. At times it may keep and add to an existing tradition. At times it descends into ruined grottoes to excavate and remove the dust from that which had lain in forgetfulness, in order to resuscitate old traditions which have the power to renew the spirit of the people.[3]

At the moment, it is absolutely essential to provide a comprehensive Jewish education that includes Israel education as a major component. A growing number of young Jews are saying that the Jewish community's failure to educate them about Israel in an honest and authentic manner has led them to disassociate from aspects of Jewish communal life. As Jewish educators, we must take these criticisms seriously. As this book will also demonstrate, in many cases, they were valid.

Our educators are also reporting a new phenomenon among young Jews. One of the realities of a post-October 7 world is that Jews can no longer hide or, at least, be discreet about their Jewishness. And this is the case at increasingly younger ages.

Regarding high school students, I have written about this as "the Anne Frank moment." It is the moment when a teacher, usually in an English or Social Studies class, teaches *The Diary of Anne Frank* to his or her students. The Jewish children, even those who have deliberately refrained from displaying their Jewishness, often have an awakening. Whether or not they want to be identified as Jewish is irrelevant. The combination of an internal spark, a presumptuous teacher's question, or a sideways glance of a classmate makes that student feel like—and become known as—the "Jewish kid."[4]

In 2023, "The Anne Frank moment" has been replaced by "the October 7 moment," and not just for Jewish students. For many Jews around the world, the days and weeks after October 7 shined the spotlight on them and awakened something within them, whether they wanted it to or not.

Thus, it does not matter whether you are motivated by the desire to improve Israel education or the fear of losing a generation of young Jews. The "October 7 moment" has happened, and as a result, Israel education must evolve—and it must evolve now.

* * *

Like all of you, I have my own journey that led me to this time and place, with an origin story that predates that devastating day of October 7.

I was born in Melbourne, Australia to a proudly Jewish and Zionist family. I attended Jewish day schools, but I really grew up in the Habonim Dror youth movement. I became an Israel educator in the 1990s, somewhat by default, after spending a year living in Israel. I got my credentials by studying for a year at Hebrew University's Senior Educator Program in 1998.

But if I were to undergo a deeper analysis, it is probably more accurate to say that my journey predates my birth. I once thought it began when my parents volunteered in Israel in the aftermath of the 1967 Six-Day War. Now, especially after a recent illuminating visit to Berlin, I think it might have begun even further back, to 1946, when my mother of blessed memory was born in the Foehrenwald Displaced Persons Camp in Germany—the daughter of a Holocaust survivor from Latvia and a partisan fighter from Poland.

After years educating in formal and informal settings in Australia and Israel, I have spent over two decades living in Brooklyn, New York, with my wife, Mirm, raising two children, Jonah (sixteen) and Abby (thirteen), and leading one of America's oldest Jewish educational institutions—The Jewish Education Project, formerly known as the Board of Jewish Education of New York.

My biography appears, implicitly and at times explicitly, throughout this book. But it was the events of October 7 and what followed that demanded I write this book. The decision to incorporate parts of myself throughout the book was partly made because I believe that you, as a reader who cares about Jewish education, will have your own stories to reflect upon as you read it. You may discover that Israel education is primarily about the individual's personal relationship and connection with Israel. Therefore, I invite you to reflect on your own Israel journey and share your experiences with friends and colleagues.

* * *

Due to my personal history, issues related to Israel and Israel education have always been immensely important to me, but as I thought and wrote about them during the summer of 2025, they became increasingly urgent.

For example, I noticed a surge in the volume and a change in the tone of news related to Israel on my social media feeds. It was a barrage of relentless images of the devastation in Gaza; endless claims of starvation, famine, ethnic cleansing, and genocide; and fleeting video footage of emaciated hostages Evyatar David and Rom Braslavski. Then there was the footage from around the world of anti-Israel rallies, including a massive march over the Sydney Harbor Bridge, Irish musicians howling "death to the IDF," and a banner at a soccer match with the words "stop killing children, stop killing civilians." Next came the leaders from around the world rushing to recognize a Palestinian state and more and more images of allegedly starving children in Gaza.

At a certain point it struck me, very hard, that if this is what my social media algorithms were serving up, just imagine what I would think if I weren't a Jewish communal professional with decades of experience educating about Israel and the Jewish people.

This realization made it clear to me who this book is for: the tens of thousands of inspiring, dedicated, and committed Jewish educators who sometimes feel confused, under-prepared, and alone, but continue guiding Jews in these unprecedented times. Along with them are the many people who make Jewish education possible. Israel education is a field with many diverse and influential stakeholders—researchers, philanthropists, educators, and most importantly the learners and their families—all of whom will be critical to forging a path forward.

They teach us that, emerging from the devastation of October 7, the Jewish people's story is still filled with heroism, pride, resilience, and survival. With the support, resources, and training they deserve, Jewish educators can continue to shape and build a thriving Jewish future, as they have done for millennia.

However, unlike much of what was thrust upon Israel and the Jewish people on and after October 7, we actually have agency over the future of Israel education. If you care enough about these issues to read this book, you likely have your own deep connection with Israel, and you are probably in a position of influence in the Jewish world. I assume that many of you are educators, and many more of you were undoubtedly impacted by educators throughout your lifetime. It falls to you to bring about the change we so desperately need.

Some of you reading this book are influencers in another sense. You are leaders in both formal and informal settings. You may serve on boards or work at foundations, communal organizations, and other nonprofits. You too are stakeholders in the Jewish educational ecosystem. Your efforts are deeply appreciated and come with significant responsibilities, as you are the ones who make Jewish education possible. As adults, many of you likely hold the most influential positions of all. You are parents, grandparents, and family members of the very young people you seek to educate.

Your concerns and responsibilities are of immense importance. However, I must say at the outset that this book is built on the premise that telling young people how to live their lives in ways we consider correct is a flawed approach. It has little chance of success in a free and democratic society. Put in positive educational language, as succinctly stated by my colleague and friend Dr. Zohar Raviv, "at its best, education must teach people how to think, and not what to think."[5]

Such an education allows learners to experience and learn something *al pi darko* (according to their way). To me, a good education means providing opportunities for learners to acquire the knowledge and skills necessary to develop their own attitudes, beliefs, and values under adverse conditions.

It is crucial to remember that Jewish educators are not responsible for solving the problems of the Jewish community or the world, although it sometimes seems as if we ask them to. Paradoxically, while Jewish educators cannot be expected to address every current issue, they do take their responsibility to shape the future of the Jewish people seriously.

Good Israel education must always be good education, a principle adopted by The iCenter, an organization that had been charged with developing the field of Israel education for the past seventeen years. It understood from the outset that, "Excellent Israel education had to be grounded in excellent education. If we miss that step, it almost doesn't matter what we're teaching."[6]

I understand that such an educational approach often makes parents and communal leaders nervous. What if our naïve children don't end up believing in the same things we do? To those people that are fearful youth will not follow in their footsteps, I suggest that we as a people must continue to have faith in our compelling story. It has survived for thousands of years and will only endure if we continue to teach what it means to be Jewish with authenticity, humanity, and morality.

Generational change has been a defining characteristic of the Jewish experience for millennia. While the changes we are currently witnessing seem to be occurring more rapidly than in the past, as is the case with many aspects of life in the modern world, Jewish educators must respond accordingly. They must provide learners with multiple pathways to help them fulfill their potential. Today, Israel plays a crucial role in this endeavor.

Just as adults have accumulated significant life experiences and embarked on diverse educational journeys, this book firmly commits to advancing an educational agenda that empowers learners to live their own lives and engage in their own learning journeys. This approach enables them to develop their own values and identities while reaching their own conclusions about the impossibly complex issues of our time. Indeed, it is likely that your beliefs today differ from those you held when you were younger; whether it was decades, years, or even weeks and days ago. This is because learning is inherently dynamic and never intended to be finite, as in the conventional approach in Israel education.

This book is divided into three main sections. The first section discusses the roles and responsibilities of Jewish educators today, especially in the context of a world after October 7. The second section consists of three chapters addressing significant issues that define today's Jewry, particularly young Jewry, and the realities Jewish educators face. The third section focuses on pedagogy and outlines five major changes with which Jewish educators will need to grapple in this new era.

Each chapter starts with a personal or professional story that introduces the main theme. This is followed by an exploration of the central problems or challenges highlighted in the episode within a broader context. The chapter then presents various perspectives that have helped me navigate these issues over the years. At the end, I attempt to make sense of the challenge for Jewish educators and may offer my viewpoint or suggestions for addressing these dilemmas. Each chapter concludes with one or more questions for further reflection and introspection, acknowledging that while this book is a marker in time, the questions it raises are perpetual and will require continuing conversation and debate.

The book addresses the field of Israel education in the two years since October 7. It argues that this era is a pivotal turning point in Jewish education, with Israel playing a crucial role due to the significant transformations experienced by Israel and the Jewish community. Admittedly, many of the suggested changes to advance the field, may have been evident to many insiders in the field of Israel education prior to October 7. But the impact of the two ensuing years now gives these needs greater voice and greater urgency. Although the full extent of October 7's impact remains uncertain, this book acknowledges the pivotal role Jewish educators often play in our communal response to such events. Educators must understand their position within this context to effectively educate, inspire, and empower the Jewish people.

You are about to discover that while some of the themes and content we must teach resemble the world of October 6, the world we live in after October 7 is vastly different for Jewish educators and those we teach. Hopefully, sharing some of my discoveries, challenges, and potential solutions will help Jewish educators navigate these new realities.

In the words of Janusz Korczak, who we shall return to later, "The one concerned with days, plants wheat; with years, plants trees; with generations, educates people."[7]

SECTION 1
The Jewish Educator in Today's World

Rabbi Abraham Joshua Heschel once said, "What we need more than anything else is not textbooks but text-people."[8] He understood that educators were a critical component in Jewish education. The empowered educator has the potential to impact all other stakeholders in the educational system, making them the primary driver of many of the necessary changes in Israel education.

The Jewish educator today comes in many forms. They are teachers in day schools and congregations, counselors at summer camps and on travel programs, *madrichim* in youth movements, professionals on college campuses, and those who work in early childhood centers and adult education programs.

Jewish educators in these settings are diverse. Some educators are paid and some are volunteers. Some hold academic degrees while others have little to no formal training. Most come to these positions with their own experiences as learners and a desire, if not a passion, to make Jewish learning meaningful and relevant.

I believe that Jewish educators must always consider themselves learners willing to embark on ongoing journeys of growth and development. Thus, the first part of this book looks at the role of the Jewish educator today through the lens of the educators' own selves, their relationship with Israel, and their burden and responsibility in telling the ongoing story of the Jewish people.

1

The Jewish Educator as Self

Over fifteen years ago, I was slated to lead a workshop about Israel education and how we begin to navigate crises with our youth. It was a CAJE[9] conference that took place in the middle of summer, just weeks just after one of the several Gaza wars had begun.

I had a beautiful PowerPoint presentation prepared. I got about five minutes into it when a brave voice said, "I can't do this. I just can't do this right now."

The screen was turned off, the lights came on, and for the next hour-and-a-half we sat there, a group of thirty or so Jewish educators, talking and maybe crying a bit as well. We simply shared how we were all feeling about the current situation and our own personal relationships with Israel.

That brave voice came from Peter Eckstein, a synagogue educator from Florida. His statement began our friendship and professional relationship, and taught me a lesson that I have never forgotten.

Peter was saying that, at any moment when Israel is in crisis, we Jewish educators jump straight into automatic pilot. We do what we are trained to do. We put our educator hats on and are there for our students. But Peter wasn't ready to put on his educator hat just yet.

From several decades of observation, I have come to believe that, in a time of crisis, educators are like all other human beings: They are often confused and unsure of their own thoughts and feelings. In Peter's case, this was because he had lived in Israel and served in the IDF. But every Jewish educator has some relationship with Israel. We cannot expect them just to go out there and teach without the opportunity to explore their own feelings about that relationship.

This is why I have long believed that Jewish educators must be given the time and space to sort out those feelings. This is not just for their sakes, but because it will make them better educators.

***

Many Jewish educators find it challenging to decide what and how much of themselves to share. While they may take a stance on a specific issue that seems to be a clear indicator of their beliefs, we must recognize that people and their opinions are constantly evolving and changing.

Sometimes these changes are triggered by major personal or collective events. For example, the first time I experienced this in regard to my relationship with Israel was when Israeli Prime Minister Yitzhak Rabin was assassinated in 1995. The second time was undoubtedly October 7.

Particularly after October 7, many educators have shifted some of their beliefs. It was a shock to many of them that their core selves came under attack on that day. For others, however, their previous beliefs were simply strengthened and affirmed.

In some ways, I can speak only for myself. So, here are a few examples of what I, as a Jewish educator, have struggled to articulate in a post-October 7 world:

- I can no longer say with full confidence that if Jewish lives are in danger, there is a country to which Jews can go and be fully protected.
- Despite the sense of solidarity in the immediate aftermath after October 7, I can no longer say with full certainty that, even when Jewish lives are threatened, the Jewish people will unite as one people with one heart and one voice.
- I can no longer say "never again" with full conviction.
- I can no longer entirely believe that freedom of speech should always be guaranteed.
- I can no longer have faith that governments around the world will protect the rights and freedoms of all their citizens.
- I can no longer say that antisemitism is marginal in the Western world.
- I can no longer be certain that there is fundamental agreement on what is good and what is evil.

These are not inconsequential statements. They go to the core of Jewish life in the twenty-first century, the foundational elements of what it means to be a Jew, including our understanding of Zionism, antisemitism, freedom, peoplehood, and humanity.

So, what happens to people, and specifically educators, when their very foundations are shaken on a single day?

Parker Palmer, a Quaker educator, wrote, "We teach who we are."[10] If this is the case, then changes of such magnitude must have a strong impact on Jewish educators. But as Palmer said, such personal crises and reassessments are, in some ways, essential to good education:

> Good teaching cannot be reduced to technique; good teaching comes from the identity and integrity of the teacher.... As I teach, I project the condition of my soul onto my students, my subject, and our way of being together. The entanglements I experience in the classroom are often no more or less than the convolutions of my inner life.[11]

Palmer's "we" could refer to more than Jewish educators. It speaks as well to the broader collective. In our case, this is the Jewish people themselves and their identity.

* * *

Israel has a profound and enduring place in the hearts and minds of many Jewish educators. For them, Israel transcends its role as a subject of instruction. It is an integral part of their identity. Conversations with Jewish educators often reveal this profound connection.

To give an example from my life, I remember the genuine excitement I felt when I awoke from my first dream in Hebrew. I eventually found out that I was not alone in feeling that such dreams are important.

Recently, I was in Israel with some colleagues. We were processing our visit to Kfar Aza and the Nova Festival site, along with our conversations with families of hostages and survivors of

October 7. Somehow, people began talking about their dreams: "You too? I haven't slept in over 100 days without having had a dream or a nightmare in which I was there on Oct. 7."

Shortly after, I gave a speech to over 150 people involved in Israel education. I asked them to raise their hands if they had similar dreams. There was silence and a sense of discomfort. Then, almost every single person raised their hand.[12]

This illustrates how deep our relationship to Israel can be embedded in our psyche. But this very intensity complicates the relationship itself. Asking oneself challenging questions and confronting one's assumptions or long-held beliefs can be difficult and certainly requires bravery. Nonetheless, the importance to Israel education of such personal honesty and integrity, especially toward ourselves, cannot be underestimated.

I have often sought to foster a relationship with the self among Jewish educators. For example, in 2014, amidst another war in Gaza, I formulated the following questions about what Israelis call the *matzav*[13]—the security situation—for Jewish educators to consider:

- When was the first time in your life that you thought about the *matzav*?
- How do you keep informed about the *matzav* in a way that advances your thinking?
- What are some of your life experiences that have challenged the way you think and feel about the *matzav*?
- When you contemplate the *matzav* today, how do you feel and what do you think?

However, I've come to realize that focusing on these types of questions only during times of crisis, war, or states of emergency is misguided because it fosters uncertainty and even distances many educators from Israel. It causes educators to take a defensive stance, whereas one of our field's responsibilities is to strive for proactive engagement. So, we must make an effort to ask these questions during times of relative calm.

This ongoing process of exploring and articulating perspectives and beliefs about Israel is essential to Jewish educators. If you support or employ a Jewish educator, it is crucial for you to provide them with the necessary space and support to engage in such reflection as an integral part of their work.

My experience has indicated that, in times of crisis, the process of self-reflection has two distinct results.

First, some people tend to reaffirm their commitment to their existing relationship with Israel. To an extent, this is the natural tendency of those who have developed their beliefs about Israel in ideologically consistent environments. Confirmation bias ensures that people often search for evidence that will support their existing beliefs. Often, they surround themselves with friends, colleagues, and social media algorithms that support and enhance their predispositions.

On the other hand, some people begin to see cracks in their existing beliefs and opinions about Israel, leading them to reexamine some of their preexisting attitudes. Such a reorientation could come after a major encounter with a differing opinion or by examining the facts in a different context. In some circles, such evolving mindsets are valued. But in other cases, this kind of "flip-flopping" is often seen as a sign of weakness.

In such cases, automatically reverting to one's prior beliefs because others expect or demand it is a mistake. The times have changed too dramatically for us to allow it. However, it is also a mistake to dismiss the long arc of Jewish history and existence because of contingent circumstances.

It is essential to remember that education does not have to mirror broader social trends. Education is meant to be a process.

It should allow for a diversity of opinions and beliefs to emerge. This is what is important, not the opinions and beliefs themselves. Education must encourage the struggle with even our most core foundational principles.

In Israel education, people often choose the first option and double down on their existing beliefs. But we are beginning to see that many Jews, including young people, are choosing to rebel, disengage, and even walk away from Israel and Jewish life as a result. Thus, reverting to traditional methods of Israel education would be a major mistake.

This is not necessarily a bad thing. Often, innovation and change become necessary because circumstances have changed so dramatically that there is no other alternative. Today, we are faced with circumstances that fundamentally challenge previous forms of Israel education. It is imperative of Jewish education in our time to confront and overcome these challenges.

* * *

Especially now, for Israel education to flourish, it is crucial for Israel educators to gain a deeper understanding of themselves. Part of this is to recognize their significance without seeing themselves as the sole focus of the classroom. This understanding—and humility—is integral to the courage to teach and the essence of being a good Israel educator today.

Confronting ourselves, especially in times of tension, is challenging, but not necessarily as challenging as asking people to articulate and share their beliefs and emotions in public.

Thus, creating safe spaces for educators to openly share their struggles free of judgment and retribution is essential, but it is not something that can be taken for granted. As Dr. Keren Fraiman has noted, there are often barriers to educators expressing their honest feelings, beliefs, and attitudes about Israel.

There are institutional pressures, of course, but educators often fear backlash from parents, administrators, and the community, or simply feel unsupported.[14]

All educators face the dilemma of how much of themselves they should share with their colleagues and their learners. Everyone's pedagogy is influenced by the self, so the question should not be how to strive for complete objectivity, but rather how forthright the educator should be with their students about their predispositions, biases, and values.

Of course, these decisions should be guided by many factors, including what is developmentally appropriate for the learners. But as Dr. Sivan Zakai reminds us, even the youngest of learners can absorb far more than many educators think.[15]

So, we end this chapter where we began, with Parker Palmer,

> Teaching, like any truly human activity, emerges from one's inwardness, for better or worse. As I teach, I project the condition of my soul onto my students, my subject, and our way of being together. The entanglements I experience in the classroom are often no more or less the convolutions of my inner life. Viewed from this angle, teaching holds a mirror to the soul. If I am willing to look in that mirror, and not run from what I see, I have a chance to gain self-knowledge and knowing myself is as crucial to good teaching as knowing my students and my subject.[16]

In these troubling times I urge all of us to hold a mirror to our souls, especially those among us privileged to be the educators of our people.[17]

Questions to Consider

- How much of the self should educators share with their learners?
- How do you grapple with situations in which your own viewpoints are in tension with the organizations you attend, participate in, or work for?

2

The Jewish Educator with Israel as Integral

In 2002, I began a two-year stint in the United States working at the Central Agency of Jewish Education in St. Louis, Missouri.

I vividly remember one of my first community education events. I was teaching at a Conservative congregation and didn't think twice about presenting a paradigm of Jewish identity that I had used dozens of times before.

As both a researcher and a teacher I had learned rather quickly that asking someone to "describe their identity" isn't a great conversation starter. So, I developed a *peulah* (activity) based on a theory of Jewish identity that is often attributed to Rabbi Abraham Isaac Kook, the first Chief Rabbi of Mandatory Palestine. I hoped this theory would help individuals uncover and articulate their own identities.

I drew a triangle and labeled each corner: The first was Torat Yisrael, the second Am (People/Nation) Yisrael, and the third Eretz (Land) Yisrael.[18] Kook's concept was that a Jew should have a relationship with the ideas described at all three corners of this triangle. So, to begin the session, I asked the participants to write their initials next to the corner that, to them, most defined their Jewish identity. (See Appendix A for a full outline of this activity.)

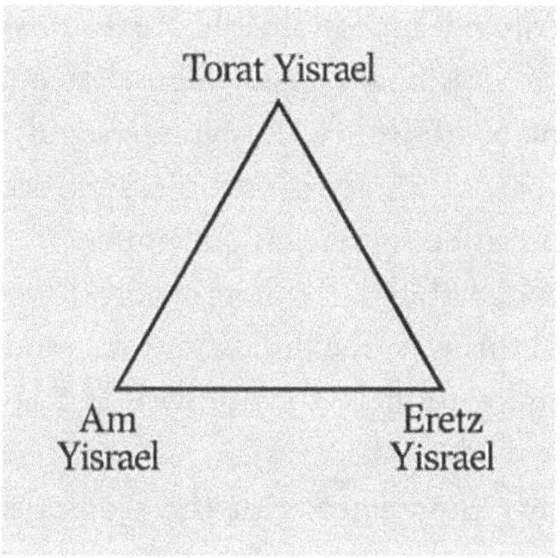

OpenAI (2026)

The audience bristled at the exercise right from the beginning. But when I stated that the term "Zionist" was synonymous with the attachment to the land that Kook described as "Eretz Yisrael" they began to audibly rumble and murmur. Then, someone finally said it out loud: "We don't feel comfortable using the term Zionist here."

Today, I understand that I had been naïve, but at the time I was taken aback. I had conducted this activity countless times before and this was the first time I had experienced pushback regarding the "Z-word." I fumbled through the rest of the session. The congregation's rabbi did try to console me afterwards, but with little success.

Nonetheless, I continued to use Kook's model many times with both Israelis and Jews around the world. While it is imperfect, it always sparks meaningful conversation.

In particular, I have noticed that people often want to add a fourth corner. Usually, it involves culture, language, family, or tradition. This often leads to valuable discussions about personal identity. Others occasionally place themselves outside the triangle entirely, not because they don't understand it, but because they don't feel part of the Jewish people. Approached with care, those moments can be significant encounters.

In short, while Rabbi Kook probably never intended his ideas to be used this way, the discussions his model has facilitated have been foundational to my growth as a Jewish and Israel educator.

However, my experience with the Conservative congregation was a wakeup call, and certainly not the last. It indicated to me that we have reached a period in Jewish history in which it can no longer to be taken for granted that Israel is critical to the identity of every Jew.

Over time, I learned that this was not only true among progressives, young people, or even Americans in general. I began to understand that twenty-first century Jewry has not inherited twentieth century paradigms of Jewish identity without question or challenge.

In the aftermath of October 7, with Zionism demonized around the world, I am in no way surprised that many people recoil at the term "Zionist." As with many other issues addressed throughout this book, these issues were prevalent before October 7. But now, they've become more critical, heated, divisive, and urgent.

Many communal discussions now focus on the divides between Zionists, non-Zionists, and anti-Zionists, and who should be included or excluded from mainstream Jewish discourse. There is a generational divide at work as well, with more and more people under the age of thirty-five labeling themselves non-Zionist or even anti-Zionist.

However, it is not my job to tell people how to label or categorize themselves. It is my job to present a better way of teaching the many expressions of Zionism.

Moreover, the issue is more complex than it appears. For example, most of the Jews I have encountered who describe themselves as non-Zionists would feel totally at home on any given Saturday night at a Tel Aviv protest. So, certain sections of the community, most notably members of what is often referred to as the "organized Jewish community," must accept some responsibility and even blame for their insistence on connecting support for Israel with support for a particular Israeli government. To ensure that Zionism can be embraced by the widest range of Jews who consider Israel an integral part of their identities, we must undo years of this miseducation.

Certainly, education must always set limits on what it considers acceptable and unacceptable. Some institutions have clearly defined boundaries that make it evident to prospective learners what they are committing to. Unfortunately, there also cases in which institutions are disingenuous and even intentionally deceptive. They promote specific ideological and partisan viewpoints and often ostracize dissenting perspectives.

This is precisely what I wish to avoid. Instead, I want an educational paradigm that helps learners define their connection to Israel by themselves. I want this because I do indeed believe that this connection is integral to Jewish identity.

Thus, I believe that our obligation as Jewish educators is to expose learners to all three components of the identity triangle of land, Torah, and peoplehood, not to convince them to adhere to any specific practice, but to empower them to make informed choices that makes sense to themselves.

* * *

A few years ago, a Jewish professional urgently called me from an airport, as the matter at hand was of utmost importance. "Bryfman," he said, "it's time we articulated a compelling reason as to why Israel should actually matter in the lives of young Jews today." It was a peculiar proposition, coming from one Zionist to another. However, considering the communal anxiety surrounding Israel at the time, it probably shouldn't have seemed so unusual.

I am not one to back off from a challenge, so I have spoken to hundreds of Jewish educators and tried on many occasions to articulate a compelling twenty-first century answer to this fundamental problem.

Often, they have responded with even more challenging questions, such as:

- Why does Israel matter if all I want to do is lead a flourishing Jewish life?
- My generation lacks a personal connection to the Holocaust, the Six-Day War, the Entebbe operation, and the rescue of Soviet and Ethiopian Jews. So why should my generation even care about Israel?
- When all one sees on the news or social media about Israel is unrest and violence, why should anyone want to be a part of that?

These questions, and many more like them, are essential to consider even before we attempt to answer the questions of why

"Israel Education Matters"[19] or "what the future of Israel education will look like."

The issue is multi-layered. On the most basic level, Israel is the center of the origin story of the Jewish people. Half and perhaps more than half of the world's Jewish population lives there. It is impossible to deny this inextricable connection to Judaism and Jewish history and culture.

On another level, however, there are the issues of the present day. Most of today's young Jews have only known an Israeli government led by Benjamin Netanyahu.[20] His right-wing governments pursue policies that are often seemingly or genuinely at odds with the values of progressive Jews—who are often young.

Interestingly, this alienation can cut both ways. I once had a conversation with a senior Israeli government official who said, "Besides [the feminist group] Women of the Wall, and the Palestinian issue, can you tell me how the actions of Israel actually impact the lives of Jews around the world?"

I met with this official again after October 7 and reminded him of the conversation. We essentially agreed that even if the question was once a real one, we now understood that Israel and world Jewry are profoundly interconnected.

Of course, the relationship between the State of Israel and Jews worldwide is not always misaligned. One of the most significant, if not the most significant, educational initiatives of Israel in the past twenty-five years, Birthright Israel, has been jointly funded by philanthropic foundations, Jewish communities globally, and the Israeli government, specifically the Prime Minister's Office.

Other Israel education initiatives have been funded by the Israeli government, most notably the Ministry of Diaspora Affairs and Combatting Antisemitism, which has set up subsidiaries to support Israel education in Jewish communities around the world.[21]

Over the years, I've been involved in numerous educational endeavors, and I owe a great deal of credit to Israeli institutions, particularly The Jewish Agency for Israel. They have been a steadfast supporter throughout my Jewish educational journey, most notably as the institution that housed the Machon Le Madrichei Chutz La'Aretz (the Institute for Youth Leaders from Abroad). In 1990, I had the privilege of participating in this program as a seventeen-year-old. Later, I studied at the Hebrew University of Jerusalem, where I first met Professor Barry Chazan and discovered the field of Israel education. This encounter profoundly changed both my personal and professional journey.

Such initiatives, which thoughtfully consider Israel's role in the development of Jewish identity—and its limits—have proven successful. They also reflect the changing relationship between Israel and Jewish communities worldwide, which were once responsible for financially supporting Israel but now, through these programs, receive Israeli taxpayer dollars.[22]

October 7 and its aftermath have convinced me that there is indeed a fourth corner to Rabbi Kook's identity model: the State of Israel, which increasingly influences, in real or perceived ways, the expression of Jewish identity around the world.

Although the term "state" has many meanings, for Jews living outside of Israel, it is most commonly associated with the Israeli government, its political leaders and legislation, and the IDF. Thus, the distinction between state and government is increasingly blurry. Unlike many people who are able to love a country regardless of who is in charge, Jews living abroad are increasingly unable to make this distinction regarding Israel.

In 2025, it's unlikely anyone would question that Israeli government decisions, statements, and policies affect Jewish religious identities worldwide (Torat Yisrael), the geography and territory that shape how Jews perceive their connection to Israel (Eretz Yisrael), and the meaning of being and expressing oneself as a Jew and a Jewish community globally (Am Yisrael). How we consider these influences will likely be an ongoing issue for Israel education in the future.

However, as Jewish educators, we can teach that governments don't represent entire populations and it is theoretically possible to love a country despite disagreeing with its policies. However, we must recognize that the young generation's information ecosystem is heavily influenced by media and social media that consistently highlight Israeli policies and actions that clash with the core values of a significant portion of Jews worldwide.

* * *

The purpose of Jewish and Israel education should not be to ensure that every learner adopts all three components of Rabbi Kook's model equally. It should be to allow for a person who is asked to "describe their Jewish identity" to do so with a more complete understanding of the possibilities available to them.

Nonetheless, I believe that Rabbi Kook's triangle is as vital today as it ever was. In this, I know that I am not "normal." Most Jewish educators, myself included, tend to identify extremely strongly with Rabbi Kook's model.

Part of the reason, for me, is the role that Torah, Am and Eretz play in my own identity. They are inextricably connected and I cannot imagine one existing without the others. Moreover, they are fluid. At various stages of my life, each corner of Rabbi Kook's triangle has taken precedence.

However, there is another element at work. There is something within me that might be described as an instinctual sense of Jewish peoplehood. My wife likes to say that I have "Jewdar," because I somehow always spot the signs of Jewish life that others don't. I see a synagogue that has been transformed into a church, the stain left behind by an old mezuza on a doorpost, a random sign on the site of the old *schmatta* (garment) stores.

I welcome the warm feeling I get at a Birthright Israel Mega Event or a JCC Maccabi opening ceremony, sitting among Jews from around the world. I know many others like me, including co-workers and colleagues. I am friends with even more on Facebook and my extended social media network.

This sense of Jewish peoplehood has often been explicitly connected to Israel and moments that can be categorized as trauma or triumph and sometimes both.

These include events that occurred even before I was old enough to remember them. Born in 1972, I have always felt some connection to the massacre of Israeli athletes at the Munich Olympic Games that year. The 1976 IDF rescue of Israeli and Jewish hostages from Entebbe airport in Uganda and the heroics of the fallen Yonatan Netanyahu have always been part of my story.

That Maccabi Tel Aviv first won the EuroLeague Basketball competition in 1977, or that "A-Ba-Ni-Bi" (1978) "Hallelujah" (1979), "Diva" (1998), and "Toy" (2018) all won the Eurovision song contest have always felt like victories to me. Watching Jews rescued from the Soviet Union and Ethiopia landing in Israel were epic events in my life, as was the awestruck feeling of meeting the great refusenik Natan Sharansky for the first time. I cried when Ilan Ramon, along with six other astronauts, died in the Space Shuttle Columbia disaster of 2003.

The assassination of Israeli Prime Minister Yitzhak Rabin on November 4, 1995 undoubtedly had the profoundest impact on my Jewish identity. For a long time, I never thought the Jewish people would recover and perhaps we never did. For me personally, the end of potential peace with the Palestinians was shattering. But more than anything, I felt that the bullets fired from Yigal Amir's gun represented the end of the collective Jewish nation as we had once imagined it to be.

I remember walking into my eighth-grade class on the Monday morning after the assassination and telling my students about Rabin's murder and how it had impacted me. I remember the tears rolling down my cheeks and a couple of thirteen-year-old boys laughing. They did not understand how the death of one man so far away could affect their teacher so intensely. Perhaps even then, I should have realized that how I experienced Israel was not the way Jewish youth experienced it. That became my primary educational challenge from then on.

Over the past two years, however, I have begun to wonder how much of an outlier I really am. An enormous number of Jews around the world were clearly devastated by the events of October 7. They have been mesmerized by Israel's incredible heroics, such as destroying Hezbollah overnight with the beeper attacks. There has certainly been some kind of awakening related to Jews' sense of connectedness to all three corners of Rabbi Kook's triangle. This presents Jewish educators with many challenges, but also many opportunities.

However, I must gently push back against my colleague Dr. Mijal Bitton, who concentrates on moments of a strong sense of Jewish peoplehood largely in moments of devastation.

Certainly, the pain she describes is very real. Moreover, the story she recounts of the "two-headed baby," originally told by Rabbi Soloveitchik, is an essential text:

> In a 1956 sermon, Rabbi Soloveitchik asks whether the dispersion of Jews across the world—and the

> ensuing diversity of Jewish customs, languages, and ways of life—has caused Jews to cease being one people: "Is the Jewish Diaspora one or not?" Are we still a "we"?
>
> To explore this question, the Rav invokes an obscure Talmudic inquiry (Menachot 37a) in which the rabbis debate the status of a man with two heads. Should he wear one or two pairs of tefillin, receive one share of inheritance, or two? The rabbis' question is legal, spiritual and ontological: They want to know whether this is a single or a multiple being.
>
> So too, the Rav asks, we should ask about the Jewish people: Are we one or many? He provides a response as profound as it is raw. He suggests that the way to determine whether the man with two heads is a single entity is to pour boiling water on one of the heads. If the other head screams in pain, then the two-headed man is a single being; if not, "then they are two individuals enfolded in one body." This painful test is the test of peoplehood. The Rav writes, "So long as there is shared suffering, in the sense of 'I am with him in his distress' (Psalms 91:15), there is unity."[23]

I must respectfully dissent from this. I believe that the attachments amongst the Jewish people around the world are not, and cannot, be built solely upon distress or tragedy. For Jewish educators, they must be established through *both* triumphs and tragedies.

Since October 7, I have spent a great deal of time giving presentations on Jewish and Israel education to communities around the world. The differences between Jewish life in the United States, South America, and South Africa are very real. The connection to Israel and Israelis are not, at least in the Jewish educational settings I encountered.

Walking around a King David School campus in Johannesburg, the senior students had prepared a school-wide commemoration of October 7. They had built a shabbat table for the hostages in the middle of the school, and a memorial that captured the spirits and lives of victims of October 7 and the ensuing war with Hamas. It was impossible to not be moved by the experience and impressed by the sensitivity, motivation, and connection that the student leaders involved in preparing for this day.

By all accounts, this type of reverence has been on display in Jewish communities around the world—in Jewish day schools, summer camps, youth groups, early childhood centers, and JCCs. These are not just acts of commemoration, but authentic expressions of connection and identity. They may have been intensified by crisis, but at other times by triumph. They are strong evidence that a Jewish peoplehood education grounded in strong and authentic connections with Israel and Israelis is both possible and desirable.

* * *

If I were tasked with providing a comprehensive Jewish education to a classroom of atheists, I would not hesitate to include God, Torah, and prayer in my curriculum. These are fundamental aspects of Jewishness, and whether the learners choose to accept, adopt, question, or reject them is largely irrelevant. I would teach them with passion and present them alongside differing viewpoints and challenging questions.

As a Jewish educator, I approach Israel with the same mindset. Today, being a Jewish educator means understanding your responsibility to offer our learners the entirety of Rabbi Kook's triangle of Jewish identity, and perhaps more.

Questions to Consider

- Today, where would you place yourself in Rabbi Kook's Jewish identity triangle?
- When have personal experiences or global events contributed to shifting your position in relation to the triangle?

3

The Jewish Educator Living History while Creating Memory

I am writing this letter to you as I am heading to the base. If you are reading it, something must have happened to me. You know me, so no one could be happier than me right now. It was no coincidence that I was on the verge of fulfilling my dream. I am happy and grateful for the privilege I will have to defend our beautiful land and the people of Israel.

In case something happens to me, I forbid you from sulking in sorrow. I've had the privilege of fulfilling my dream and destiny and you can be certain that I am looking down on you with a huge smile. I will probably sit next to grandpa and catch up on what we've missed, each of us will share our experiences and what's changed between the wars. Maybe we'll also talk a little politics, and I'll ask him what he thinks.

If God forbid you are sitting shiva [the week of mourning], transform it into a week of friends, family, and fun. There should be good food, meat of course, beer, soft drinks, nuts, and of course mom's cookies. Tell jokes, share stories, and you'll get to meet all the rest of my friends that you haven't yet met. You know? I envy you. I would want to sit there and see everyone.

Another matter that is very, very important. If God forbid, I fall into captivity, dead or alive, I will not allow a single soldier or citizen to be harmed because of some bargaining made for my release. I forbid you to conduct a campaign or struggle or anything of the sort. I am not willing to have terrorists released for me. In no way, shape or form. Don't misconstrue my words please.

I'll say it again; I left the house without even being called up to reserve duty. I am filled with pride and a sense of purpose and I always said that if I have to die, I wish it would be in defense of others and the State. "Jerusalem, I have placed guards, that one day will come and I will be one of them."[24]

This is a letter written by Israeli soldier Ben Zussman, to be sent only in case of his death or capture. On December 3, 2023, he was killed in Gaza.

When I met with Ben's mother Sarit Zussman as part of a group of Jewish educators, her words were simple and profound, "I would love for people to hold the love that Ben felt—love for the country and its people.... Do whatever you can, but do it with a smile...live, laugh, eat well, sit together...be alive."[25]

Over the past two years, Jewish educators have heard numerous testimonies, such as Ben's final letter and Sarit's moving words, from individuals directly affected by the events of October 7 and the ensuing war. Many educators have traveled to Israel, visited the sacred grounds of the Nova Festival site, met with families of hostages and hostages themselves, and paid *shiva* calls to the families of Israeli soldiers fallen in battle. Educators have closely followed events over the past two years via the media and social media, likely with an unprecedented level of interest.

Previous chapters have encouraged educators to reflect on their identities and consider the role Israel should play in their educational philosophy. Those chapters could have been written before October 7. This chapter specifically urges us to examine how the experiences of the past two years have affected us not just as individuals, but as Jewish educators. Our responsibility is to ensure that Ben Zussman's story and legacy, along with those of thousands of others, are preserved as part of Jewish memory.

* * *

1948. 1956. 1967. 1973. 1982. 1987. 2000. 2006.[26]

These dates, marking various Israeli wars and conflicts, are familiar to many Jewish educators. We can now add 2023 and the twelve-day war with Iran in July 2025. Though many Jewish educators have recounted the history of Israel largely through these conflicts, this must not continue to be the case. However, before we as educators work together to establish a more comprehensive curriculum for Israel education, we should take stock of the past two years.

October 7 and its aftermath will loom large in Israeli and Jewish history. It may prove to be an inflection point in the ongoing evolution of the Jewish people. So, I ask all Jewish educators: What does it mean to be living at a historic moment? I ask all educators who have traveled to Israel since October 7: What does it mean to bear witness to these times?

These are not new questions. Many have sought to answer them. Since October 7, there has been no shortage of answers. Numerous people have written about the significance of this moment. Many have acknowledged the overwhelming responsibility that lies ahead for all of us as a result.[27]

But for Jewish educators, there is an additional question. It is, in some ways, unprecedented: As an educator, what does it mean to witness a historic moment while being simultaneously entrusted with the responsibility of creating Jewish memory?

I am not the first to note the difference between Jewish history and Jewish memory. History is usually defined as the study of past events, while memory is constructed from the past to shape the present and future. The historian Yosef Hayim Yerushalmi wrote in his seminal book *Zachor*, "Jewish memory was always a deep source of meaning, sustained not by critical history but by ritual, liturgy, and legend."[28]

Rabbi Lord Jonathan Sacks wrote,

> Smartphones and tablets have developed even larger memories, while ours and those of our children have become smaller and smaller. Why bother to remember anything if you can look it up in a microsecond on Google or Wikipedia? But this confuses history and memory, which are not the same thing at all. History is an answer to the question, "What happened?" Memory is an answer to the question, "Who am I?" History is about facts; memory is about identity. History is about something that happened to someone else, not me. Memory is my story, the past that made me who I am, of whose legacy I am the guardian for the sake of generations to come. Without memory, there is no identity, and without identity, we are mere dust on the surface of infinity.[29]

Like many Jewish educators around the world, I vividly remember my first encounter with Avraham Infeld. Calling it a "lecture" hardly captures the experience. It was more like a transformative moment. Infeld, a distinguished Jewish educator and leader, commanded the room with his booming South African-accented voice. I later realized that whether he was speaking to twenty students or a thousand audience members, his speech was always the same:

> Jews don't have history. We have memory. History is about what happened. Memory is about what happened to me. The Jewish people remember events not just as past occurrences, but as experiences that continue to shape our identity today. We left Egypt. We stood at Sinai. We were exiled from Jerusalem. These are not stories about "them"—they are stories about "us." That's the power of Jewish memory. It binds us together as a people and gives our identity meaning beyond time and geography.[30]

Today, it is critical to grasp the distinction between history and memory. As we emerge from these historic times, Jewish educators are tasked with creating the enduring memory of events.

When we talk about October 7 in the years to come, educators will be making clear choices as to what we convey about these events and how we convey it. To paraphrase Rabbi Sacks and Infeld, it is already clear that even if Jews around the world were not directly impacted by October 7, the events of that day and its aftermath happened to *us*, and not to someone else. As we continue to remember and teach about those events, we are also actively creating a collective memory for generations to come.

This is not the first time educators have been tasked with creating memory. In many societies, storytelling is recognized as a crucial component of this process. As Jews, we have a long tradition of educators using stories of our past to nurture contemporary identity. Maurice Halbwachs wrote extensively on this subject.[31] J.V. Wertsch explicitly described educational settings (mainly schools), as "among the most powerful institutions for shaping collective memory, often working in concert with textbooks, museums, and rituals to produce national narratives."[32] Aleida Assmann has suggested that, "Educational institutions are the key carriers of cultural memory. They stabilize, transmit, and renew memory by selecting what is worth remembering."[33]

As Jewish educators, we are tasked with both remembering October 7 and shaping the collective memory of the past two years. This involves more than just considering how Yom HaZikaron (Israel's Memorial Day) will be observed next year, though we understand that rituals and commemorations are crucial to creating collective memory. It is too early to establish permanent rituals to memorialize October 7, but discussions are already underway on how this day and its aftermath will be remembered.

Forms of remembrance always change and develop. It took many years before Yom HaShoah (Holocaust Remembrance Day) became what it is today. Soon, no Holocaust survivors will be left alive, and thus commemorations will undergo a dramatic transformation. Moreover, remembrance of the Holocaust (and fallen Israeli soldiers) should not be confined to a single day each year.

For some people, their connection to Israel since October 7 feels visceral and immediate. They may have family there, visited the country, or built strong relationships with Israelis over the years. For many young Jews, however, Israel remains more of an abstract concept. It is a place they've learned about but have yet to experience firsthand.

How we teach about October 7 and its aftermath will not only provide these learners with historical facts, stories, and information. It will shape their relationship with Israel as well. This is also part of collective memory. So, when educators consider our role in shaping the individual and collective memory of October 7, we must recognize that we have a crucial responsibility to the Jewish people.

It's not too early for educators to start reflecting on the values they want to impart via commemorations of October 7. This will be a complex task. As Dr. Ben Jacobs, associate research professor at George Washington University, wrote, "The classic 'march through time' approach that begins with the details of the remote past simply does not interest or motivate the majority of today's youth.... A more relevant and responsive approach would be to center the curriculum on present-day concerns from which students can trace historical roots."[34]

We should already be explicitly addressing these diverse "present-day" concerns and questioning why we prioritize certain narratives and incidents over others. During my visits to schools over the past two years, I observed that one school dedicated a large space to honoring soldiers like Ben Zussman, who sacrificed their lives defending the Jewish state. Another school highlighted acts of heroism from October 7, specifically sharing the stories of female soldiers who conducted surveillance over Gaza, Bedouins who risked their lives to save people from the Nova site, and Rachel, who offered cookies to terrorists when they invaded her home in Ofakim. One educator focused on the beeper attack that eliminated a significant number of Hezbollah terrorists. Another primarily spoke about Vivian Silver, a Canadian-born Israeli who spent decades promoting Arab-Jewish cooperation and social justice and was killed in the Be'eri massacre.

These examples show that the messages educators choose to share in a post-October 7 world reflect the experiences that were most powerful to them personally. However, these messages also shape how October 7 will be remembered by future generations.

* * *

I have struggled to find the right words for this moment in history. Previously, I described October 7 as the twenty-first century's defining moment for the Jewish people. I also call it "the Jewish peoplehood moment of our times." It might be too soon for such labels, but I believe that acknowledging the massive impact of October 7 and its aftermath in Israel and for Jews worldwide is crucial, even now.

For Jewish educators, this is an enormous responsibility. Jewish educators have long been committed to teaching our collective history. Today, however, it is not just a common history that they must convey, but also our common present and common destiny.

In the days following October 7, I realized the immense responsibility I faced and began reaching out to close colleagues and friends in Israel. They were in shock. Many were angry. All were traumatized. Despite this, they had work to do. They had to try to make sense of October 7 in real time. Their efforts during this period were crucial in helping me not only to understand the events educationally but also develop essential educational strategies and actions to guide me through these challenging times.

In the wake of October 7, I sought guidance from Dr. Zohar Raviv, the international vice president of educational strategy at Taglit-Birthright Israel. Our first meeting had taken place at a cemetery in Newport, Rhode Island long before the events of

October 7. Even then, he conveyed valuable insights into identity and memory.

Zohar has long emphasized that Jewish educators are custodians of collective memory, choosing what to remember and how to pass it on.[35] He also believes that, while our tragedies must be remembered, that they cannot become the foundations by which we establish our identities as Jews.[36] He urges that, as Jews, we must move beyond victimhood toward resilience and contribution. In the aftermath of October 7, he stated cthat educators must act immediately and strategically to shape a vision that preserves memory and also guides future generations:

> We uphold the seminal need to be wholly reactive to these events, while remaining strategically proactive in realizing the fuller potential of solid Jewish and Israel education in the broadest sense.... We wish to articulate a strategic blueprint whose impact not only functions visàvis October 7 but extends far beyond that day.[37]

This reminds me of one of the first recorded Passover seders, which is recounted every year via the Haggadah: "It happened that Rabbi Eliezer, Rabbi Yehoshua, Rabbi Elazar ben Azariah, Rabbi Akiva, and Rabbi Tarfon were reclining in Bnei Brak and discussing the Exodus all that night."[38] I think it's safe to assume that, when these five rabbis were reclining and discussing, they didn't think that the account of their evening together would be told and retold, over and over again, for thousands of years.

Today, there are more than five people telling a story together. There are thousands of educators, rabbis, academics, and communal leaders telling the stories of October 7 again and again. These servants of the Jewish people are not just telling stories. At their best, they are constructing experiences and creating memory.

In all likelihood, the collective memory of October 7 will be constructed differently in Israel and for Jews living outside of Israel.

For Jews around the world, forming a collective memory of October 7 will likely start by establishing spaces—educational, communal, and ritual—where stories, testimonies, and emotions can be identified, processed, and preserved. Memory will be shaped through carefully designed curricula, narratives from survivors and responders, commemorative activities in schools and synagogues, artistic and cultural expressions, and opportunities for global Jews to reflect on what the day revealed about vulnerability, solidarity, antisemitism, and Jewish identity.

The goal should not only be to maintain historical accuracy but also to ground Jewish identity in the moral and communal responsibilities that arose from the attack. These responsibilities include the need for mutual support, the courage to speak out, and the duty to support Israelis in their ongoing trauma and recovery.

For Israelis, the collective memory of October 7 will be forged more through a lived experience of rupture, personal loss, national trauma, civic failure, heroism, and societal resilience. It will be shaped by state commemorations, school curricula, military and civilian testimonies, public inquiries, memorial sites, cultural production, and the ways families and communities narrate their own experiences of fear, survival, and grief.

It is likely that this collective memory will become a central axis of national identity. It will influence security doctrine, political discourse, social cohesion, and debates about the future of Israeli democracy and Jewish-Arab relations. It will be carried in bodies as much as in books. It will be a wound, a warning, and a source of moral reckoning.

Together, these two trajectories could form a unified collective memory of October 7, one that honors the lived pain in Israel and the profound reverberations felt across the Jewish world. Religious leaders will play an essential role in constructing this memory, but it is essential for educators to play a role as well, partly because so many of the victims of October 7 were not religious. Jewish educators will be essential to weaving these narratives into a shared framework, ensuring that October 7 becomes not only a story of tragedy but a catalyst for renewed peoplehood, ethical responsibility, and a collective commitment to the Jewish future.

Zohar Raviv once presented a challenge to Jewish educators: to move from being storytellers to story-bearers. "A story-bearer," Zohar says, "asks themselves: what is my personal stake in the story? What is my vested interest in the story? They add their values and beliefs as they share the story with others. They reach a state of mind and heart where they experience the story and develop a profound interest in the outcome of the story."[39]

The Jewish educator has long been tasked with being a teacher of Jewish history, but their responsibility has always been greater than just teaching facts. In a post-October 7 world, as Jewish educators move from being storytellers to story-bearers, they will use the history we are living to create the collective memory of generations to come. That is both our responsibility and our obligation.

Questions to Consider

- In what ways have specific historical events impacted your life and your identity?
- In what ways has October 7 affirmed or changed your identity?
- What are the stories of October 7 that you are choosing to share and to bear?

SECTION 2
The Evolving World

During the Gaza War of 2014, a group of very anxious parents of Jewish tweens approached me. Due to my role directing the teen department of The Jewish Education Project, they asked me to promote a campaign to discourage Jewish children from accessing social media.

The parents' argument was simple: If children did not encounter the barrage of online attacks on Israel, they would not be upset or swayed by them. Without diminishing their role as parents, I told them in no uncertain terms that I thought it was a bad idea. Moreover, even if it were a good idea, the power of social media was too strong to be stopped.

In the end, these parents were faced with three choices:

1. Ban their children from using social media.
2. Impose a filtering or monitoring system in order to control the social media content their children consume.
3. Teach their children to screen and filter content.

Even though in 2025 Australia introduced a world-first law restricting social media for kids under sixteen years of age, in my view, the third is the only viable option for our sub-community of Jewish educators, as imperfect and frustrating as it may be.

This speaks to larger issues at play: The evolution of knowledge, surging antisemitism, and growing divisiveness in various societies. All of them are impacting Jewish and Israel education.

We must accept that we cannot control these forces. They are too powerful. Nevertheless, as Jewish educators, we can empower our learners to comprehend and confront them.

4

Evolving Knowledge

In 1996, I worked with two wonderful fifteen-year-old students who were competing in the international "3000 Jerusalem Quiz," part of a celebration marking Jerusalem's 3,000th anniversary. They both studied diligently, won the Australian competition, and reached the final round. They traveled to Israel to compete in the one-time event, which in Israel was on the same level as the annual International Bible Quiz that screens on national television on Israel's Independence Day. The students' studies fostered a palpable attachment between them and the eternal capital of the Jewish people.

This part of my educational journey comes to mind due to the event's emphasis on facts and knowledge. In the case of the Jerusalem Quiz, gaining more information strengthened the students' connections to Jerusalem. However, it is important to remember that both girls already had strong emotional ties to Israel, which clearly motivated them to begin their learning journey.

As the People of the Book, Jews have always valued knowledge. In the aftermath of October 7, however, much of the Jewish world became more obsessed with it than ever. This was mainly due to the upheaval occurring on college campuses in North America and around the world. Many in the Jewish community were shocked by the violent anti-Israel protests, university administrations' inability or unwillingness to control them, and Jewish students' confusion as to how to respond.

My inbox was inundated with requests for programs and initiatives to "fill our kids with more of the right knowledge" about Israel. Initially, I was surprised by these suggestions because my career has primarily focused on experiential Jewish education. I have often emphasized the affective and behavioral aspects of Jewish educational experiences rather than just the acquisition of information. Although I have consistently argued that effective experiential education does not have to compromise cognitive learning, it is evident that summer camps, youth groups, Israel trips, and other informal Jewish settings prioritize *doing* and *feeling* over *knowing* about Jewish and Israel-related content.

Perhaps I was wrong all those years. Perhaps my emphasis on *doing* rather than *knowing* contributed to those besieged college students' lack of knowledge. Perhaps we Jewish educators simply didn't get the balance right.

This focus on what is often referred to as the ABCs (Affect, Behavior, Cognition) of education has received renewed attention in the Jewish community since October 7. Jonathan Golden has presented a compelling perspective on this through his theory of the "Heart, Head, Hands" of Israel education: "Heart: How do I feel? Head: What do I want to know? Hand: What might I want to do?"[40]

Educators recognize the necessity of all three components in Jewish education. Nonetheless, one of the most prevalent critiques following October 7 was the perceived knowledge gap within the Jewish community regarding Israel and Zionism. Many argued that if our children had been better informed, they would have been better equipped to handle the onslaught of anti-Israel rhetoric they encountered on social media, in classrooms, and from their peers.

Before we rush to conclude that the solution to a supposedly ignorant Jewish student population is simply to provide them with more information, we should consider the rest of Golden's argument. Along with his assertion that all three components are essential to effective Israel education, he emphasizes the importance of the order in which they are presented: "For some learners, especially teens, feeling connected or acting meaningfully can come before they fully understand the nuances. The learning (head) catches up later."[41]

All of this is important, but today, I have come to believe that when it comes to Israel and the Middle East, Jewish educators need to know more of the right stuff.

* * *

The concept of the *right stuff* is familiar to many Jewish educators. It is often referred to as "Jewish literacy." There have been several attempts to construct models and outcomes for Jewish literacy,[42] but very few for Israel education specifically.

One of the challenges of developing a literacy framework for Israel education is the distinct nature of each educational setting. The idea of creating a knowledge base relevant to a youth group at a JCC, an Orthodox Jewish day school, and a Reform Jewish summer camp all at the same time seems implausible. However, these rationales often serve as excuses. They imply that learning the same facts is impossible in such diverse settings. This is untrue.

Communal leaders often concentrate mainly on Jewish day schools as the main venue for young people to learn about Israel. It is true that Jewish day schools are an excellent setting for acquiring knowledge about Israel, and due to the extensive hours available for teaching, they may be the most effective. A communal approach to Israel education, however, particularly for increasing young people's knowledge about Israel, must be implemented in other settings. This is important if only because the majority of Jewish youth worldwide do not attend Jewish day schools.

There is also a tendency to argue about the appropriate age for learners to acquire specific information. This is an excuse, or at least a distraction, as all educators recognize that the construction of any curriculum must always be developmentally appropriate.

Despite these caveats, I believe that once an educational organization recognizes the importance of learning more about Israel, it might discover more similarities across Jewish educational settings than initially thought. It can do so by asking a few basic questions.

While these questions are not the only ones to consider, I believe they can be helpful as a guide. They can establish a baseline for assessing what learners need to know about Israel.

- What are the pivotal moments in time that established the Jewish people's connection to the Land of Israel?
- What are the various texts that describe the ways different Jews have felt connected with the Land of Israel over thousands of years?
- What do various maps teach me about the Jewish people and others' connection to the Land of Israel and the Middle East?
- What sources of information give me a better understanding of the broad diversity of people who live in and around Israel today?

- What are some of the key sources that define Israel as both a Jewish state and a democracy?

Especially after October 7, questions like these—with a strong focus on knowledge—have provided me with a perspective I hadn't had before. I always assumed that if people had positive feelings about and positive associations with Israel, learning the *right stuff* would naturally follow. However, October 7 revealed that this assumption is not only false but also that stronger connections with Israel can be achieved through a solid foundation of knowledge.

One of the most persuasive data points regarding the need of more Israel knowledge, especially for today's younger generation, comes from the research conducted by the newly formed non-profit organization Boundless.[43] One striking result of their research relates to the term "Zionism." The data indicates that when Jewish students receive a clear, values-based definition of Zionism, they are more likely to feel connected to it and express support for it, particularly in environments where Zionism is frequently misunderstood, misrepresented, or maligned:

> In a 2023–24 study of college students, 42% of the sample had either never heard of the term Zionism or had heard it but didn't know what it meant. Before a definition was offered 31% of respondents self-identified as a Zionist. The following definitions of Zionism given to the students:
>
> *"Zionism is a movement that supports the Jewish people having a state in their ancestral homeland, Israel."*

> *"Anti-Zionism is a movement that does not believe the Jewish people should have a state in their ancestral homeland, Israel."*
>
> After offering these definitions the share of students identifying as Zionist rose from 31% to 53%—a +22-percentage point shift.[44]

It is important to recognize that people's identities are often transformed as they acquire more knowledge. For example, Harold Himmelfarb distinguishes Jewish identification from Jewish identity. He posits that *identification* refers to observable behaviors and affiliations that indicate involvement in Jewish life, such as ritual practice or organizational participation. By contrast, *identity* refers to a person's internal sense of self, the subjective meaning and emotional significance of being Jewish. Thus, someone may display high identification without deep identity or possess strong identity with minimal external behavior.[45] Knowledge is essential to how these two models develop.

The questions mentioned above are all based in acquiring knowledge. But a good teacher doesn't stop at answering those questions. The good Jewish educator knows that they are the basis of deeper questions of purpose, meaning, and connection—in other words, identity and identification.

As we discussed earlier, the debate over the primary focus of Israel education is a real one. Some have suggested that the true subject of Israel education is the learner's evolving relationship with Israel, while others argue that it is Israel itself.[46] This artificial dichotomy is unhelpful, and educators don't have to make a binary choice. To be effective, a good Israel educator must prioritize both the subject matter and the learner's relationship with Israel.

By gaining a deeper understanding of the land and people of Israel, learners can strengthen their own personal connection to Israel. This connection allows them to see themselves as part of the evolving Jewish story, rather than separate from it.

* * *

Beyond the answers to the questions above, what do Jewish youth need to know about Israel? In September 2024, I wrote "A Canon for Israel Education" that attempted to answer this question:

"A Canon for Israel Education."[47]

> One purpose of Jewish education is to prepare Jewish people for the world in which they live. The events of Oct. 7 and its aftermath have shaken many of my educational foundations to the core, including the explicit need for Jewish youth to "know more stuff" about Israel. Why? Because to be a Jew in the world today requires a connection to Israel that is based on attitudes (heart) and behaviors (hands) in addition to knowledge (head).[48]
>
> With that in mind, I would like to share twelve fundamentals that all Jewish youth living outside of Israel (and perhaps in Israel too) need to familiarize themselves with to establish their baseline foundational knowledge about Israel. Think of it as the beginning of a canon for Israel education.
>
> To be clear, this is not an attempt to outline everything about Israel education—there are many additional things that we will want our youth to encounter and

learn from in the course of building a relationship with the Jewish homeland. Instead, this is an acknowledgment that Jewish education needs to help our young people know more about Israel.[49]

Prior to the age of bnei mitzvah

1. *Genesis* 12:1

The beginning is a very good place to start. The story of Avram being promised the Land of Israel is a critical foundation story for our young children to know, as this is the origin story of the Jewish people's connection to their homeland.[50]

2. Passover Haggadah

Our children must learn that Pesach is the festival of freedom, not just the "Festival of Spring." The Israelite journey from slavery to freedom culminates in entering the Land of Israel.

Along with the Four Questions and the Ten Plagues, children should explicitly learn that the Passover Seder culminates with the phrase, "Next year in Jerusalem." Over the last few decades, there have been countless Haggadot and supplemental readings that seek to universalize this text or even this exact phrase. That is wonderful, but this content should not come at the expense of passages of a particularistic nature.[51]

3. 'Hatikvah'

Na'ase v'nishma. "We will do and then we will listen." We teach our children to sing, and then we should educate them about the words of the Israeli national anthem. It is not only an anthem but a song about hope, one that expresses and reinforces our 2,000-year-old collective past with our shared destiny "to be a free people in our own land."[52]

4. Map of Israel

At an early age, the map of Israel is as much a symbol as it is a geography lesson. While the map itself will take on different significance as learners develop, maps provide an opportunity for even young learners to familiarize themselves with key cities, sites, and various people inhabiting the land.[53]

5. "Yerushalayim Shel Zahav" ("Jerusalem of Gold")

The classic Naomi Shemer song is a powerful way to combine the teaching of history, tradition, and culture that expresses the connection of the Jewish people to Jerusalem.

6. Hebrew

The earlier we instill in our youth that Hebrew is a vibrant and living language, the greater appreciation they will have for Israeli culture, the Jewish people, and our rich textual tradition. I suggest that that every young Jew should learn at least one hundred conversational Hebrew phrases.[54]

In the teenage years

7. Declaration of Independence

This is a quintessential document that all Jews should be familiar with. The preamble alone provides an essential understanding of Jewish and Zionist history, while the following paragraphs (especially paragraph thirteen) provide a blueprint for the Jewish state we should continually strive for.[55]

8. Law of Return

One cannot fully understand Zionism and Jewish peoplehood without understanding this foundational law of the Jewish state. On the basic level, this law is important to Israel because it grants Jews, people of Jewish ancestry, and their spouses the right to immigrate to Israel and become citizens. But on a deeper level, the law is the rationale for contemporary Zionism: the need for Jews to have a land of their own, a safe haven, and a political state like all other national entities.[56]

9. Zionist thinkers

Our youth should be familiar with the origins of political Zionism and Theodor Herzl's *The Jewish State*. Advancing this conversation should also include an understanding of the diversity of Zionist thought and the diversity of the country's population. The writings of Ahad Ha'am, Ze'ev Jabotinsky, Rav Kook, and Berl Katznelson represent the history, cultural context, and various motivations of the Zionist movement, all of which are foundations for understanding Zionism today.[57]

10. The other maps of Israel

At the very least, our youth must know about the 1947 Partition Plan and the maps of 1948 and 1967. Maps show much more than city names, borders, and terrain. It is imperative that our youth understand the armistice lines, green lines, and red lines of Israeli history before they go out into the world and need to utilize this information.[58]

11. Palestinian nationalism

There is no doubt that reading documents related to Palestinian nationalism will be challenging for Jewish youth, but to forfeit any attempt to understand the other actors in the Israeli-Palestinian context would be a failure of Israel education.[59] Suggested reading includes the Palestinian National Charter (1968), the Hamas Charter (1987), excerpts from Edward Said's *Orientalism* (1978), or Rashid Khalidi's *The Hundred Years War on Palestine*. Better that our youth first encounter these perspectives in a Jewish educational setting than in an antagonistic context.

12. Culture from contemporary Israeli artists

As recently demonstrated by the wide usage of Eden Golan's Eurovision song "Hurricane (October Rain)" by many in Jewish education and the arts, writing, visual art and music should be part of the knowledge base that we instill in our young people. The arts are often the great texts of our time, expressed through different mediums, and they can provide young people with windows into Israel that other vehicles cannot.[60]

Too many Jews are ignorant of these foundational resources related to Israel. Thankfully, with the right educators, Jewish youth can learn about these things in different ways, in different educational settings, and at appropriate stages of development. I invite you to debate with me and add and subtract resources of your own.

Consider what it would look like if we raised a generation of young people to both hold opinions and have their beliefs grounded in knowledge and context. Knowledge acquisition is a cornerstone of all good education, and Jewish and Israel education should provide nothing less.

* * *

I believe that knowing more about Israel is fundamentally a good thing, but it is also important to acknowledge that simply acquiring more knowledge about Israel may not necessarily lead to a stronger connection to the Jewish state.

Some Jewish educators are concerned that learning about potentially controversial events in Israel's past might negatively impact a learner's connection to Israel. While it is true that learning about historical events from "the other side" could be unsettling for Jewish learners, Jewish educators must expose Jewish learners to various Palestinian narratives when developmentally appropriate.

As uncomfortable as it might make educators feel, it is far better that they be exposed to this accounting of history for the first time in a safe and trusted environment. Over time, we have seen that young people hearing terms like "nakba"[61] and learning about events like those that occurred at Deir Yassin[62] and Sabra and Shatilla[63] in non-Jewish and sometimes antagonistic environments have left Jewish youth wondering why they were not taught about these events in Jewish contexts.

Some young adults claim that their Jewish educators deliberately shielded them from certain things due to concerns that they did not align with the Jewish and Zionist narrative. This has even prompted some students to create a website compiling anecdotes about moments they felt misled by their educators. A *Tablet* magazine article on this phenomenon states:

> It says that our Jewish day schools, our summer camps, our synagogues, and our youth groups intentionally told us something untrue: that the State of Israel is beyond reproach; that when the country was established it was on bare, empty land; that the Palestinian people are nothing but a band of bloodthirsty terrorists. This line of thought maintains that, while we were raised to think Israel is good and gentle, a Jewish safe space, in truth the country is actually evil and committing myriad war crimes, and it's like *totally* apartheid. In this new telling, our Jewish day schools, our summer camps, our synagogues, and youth groups were all well-oiled lie and propaganda machines covering up the dark truth about the Jewish nation: namely, that Israel is a villainous colonial project that is barbarous toward its true natives and probably the worst abuser of human rights in the world.[64]

Over time, I have faced significant pushback when I promote the inclusion of Palestinian voices in Jewish education. Despite the difficulties some may experience in incorporating these perspectives, the events of October 7 have further convinced me that it is essential.

I would argue that excluding Palestinian voices is a dereliction of duty on the part of Jewish educators. We should include these voices not because we want Jewish youth to be drawn to them—though they might be—but because effective Israel education must adhere to fundamental critical educational practices. This includes exposing learners to diverse narratives so they can reach their own conclusions and because it is important to ensure that they are not first exposed to these narratives in potentially antagonistic environments.

Today, I believe that including Palestinian voices in Israel education is less controversial than it previously was in many, but not all, Jewish educational settings, although I acknowledge it is not universally implemented. In other chapters, I address some of the other challenging issues that face Israel educators today, such as racism and the rise of authoritarianism in Israel, and more recent accusations of famine and genocide against the Israeli government.

* * *

In any discussion about the role of knowledge in Israel education, perhaps the most critical question for Jewish educators to consider is whether we are prepared for today's knowledge revolution.

For many Jewish educators, it feels like they were introduced to Google and Wikipedia just yesterday. However, it is essential to understand the advantages and risks of today's knowledge revolution. For example, a recent Wikipedia definition of Zionism highlights one of the main problems with today's technology, which is often shaped by the "wisdom" of the masses rather than by experts:

> Zionism is an ethnocultural nationalist movement that emerged in late 19th-century Europe to establish and support a Jewish homeland through the colonization of Palestine, a region corresponding to the Land of Israel in Judaism and central to Jewish history. Zionists wanted to create a Jewish state in Palestine with as much land, as many Jews, and as few Palestinian Arabs as possible.[65]

Jewish educators have also begun to consider—and worry about—the role played by social media, influencers, and artificial intelligence in creating and distributing Israel-related content.

I worry about these things myself for many reasons. For example, I once asked a group of twelfth-grade students in a South African Jewish day school if they had ever heard of the term "nakba." They stared at me blankly until one said that she had recently heard about it on TikTok.

There are many other instances of the malign influence of technology: Influencer Dua Lipa denounced "Israeli genocide" in an Instagram post and called on her 88 *million* followers to "show your solidarity with Gaza" following an Israeli attack on Rafah.[66] Anti-Defamation League researchers found that ChatGPT incorrectly stated that there was no credible information that Hamas murdered babies during the October 7 attack.[67] In another study, ChatGPT provided significantly higher fatality estimates when asked about Israeli airstrikes in Arabic rather than Hebrew.[68]

In today's world, the influence of Jewish educators in imparting knowledge about Israel might seem to pale into insignificance compared to other information sources. Thus, it is crucial to invest in Jewish organizations that use technology to promote the spread of positive information about Israel, because technology is how young people learn and information is disseminated in the twenty-first century.

A few years ago, someone suggested to me that significant Jewish communal investment should be made in editing all Jewish-related Wikipedia pages, because they were the primary source of Jewish information for most people, including Jews, at the time. This proposal had significant issues, as manipulating Wikipedia can be illegal depending on the method and intent. Nonetheless, stakeholders in Jewish education have much to gain from understanding this new knowledge frontier. This includes recognizing that the forces shaping online and social media content are much larger and often more sinister than any coordinated effort by the Jewish community could ever be.

* * *

So, where does this leave us? The truth is, we live in a world where too many people have opinions about things they know very little about. As Zohar Raviv says, we are "navigating the age of informed ignorance."[69]

Thus, Jewish educators have no choice but to embark on a dual mission. First, we must do our utmost to teach Jewish learners as much as possible about Israel and Zionism. We should teach in dynamic and sophisticated ways. We ought to calibrate this learning to the various ages and settings in which Jewish learners gather. But simply put, we need to create generations of Jews who are "Israel literate."

Second, and no less important, we must teach our learners how to navigate the vast world of knowledge and information they inhabit. We should teach them how to evaluate media sources and obtain information from multiple perspectives, both to know what others are thinking and to affirm or challenge some of their assumptions. All of this is essential to good Israel education.

Questions to Consider

- What are your competence and confidence levels regarding your own knowledge about Israel?
- Where do you currently get most of your knowledge and information about Israel, and how might these sources be multiplied and diversified?

5

Evolving Antisemitism

In 2018, a group of us were conducting research at The Jewish Education Project. We oversaw some focus group discussions with Jewish teens from around the United States.[70] We were able to interview several teenagers about their perspectives on the recent shooting at the Tree of Life Synagogue in Pittsburgh in which eleven people attending a Shabbat morning service were murdered.

We asked the teens to reflect on the tragedy. Most shared their sense of how frightening it is to be Jewish in the world today.

What surprised us, however, was that a significant number stated that they did not feel the shooting was necessarily antisemitic. They pointed to attacks on other minority groups—LGBTQ people, Muslim, Sikhs, and so on—as evidence that this was just another tragic example of extremist racism and gun violence in America. One teen went as far to suggest that we were privileging hatred of Jews over hatred of other marginalized groups.

I told this story to the scholar Deborah Lipstadt, who later became the *US Department of State Special Envoy to Monitor and Combat Antisemitism.* She dismissed this evidence of generational ignorance. "Jews were targeted and killed in synagogue on Shabbat. How is there any doubt that this was antisemitism?" she asked.

I recount this story to illustrate that although the aftermath of October 7 unquestionably marked a shift in our confrontation with antisemitism, many of the issues that this chapter raises existed long before. As I write this book, it is too soon to tell, but my solid hunch is that even the most progressive Jewish teenagers today would see attacks on Jews praying in Manchester and celebrating in Sydney as distinctly antisemitic—even if they include caveats regarding some connection to what is transpiring in Israel.

This chapter is one I never thought I would need to write. Even a few years ago, I could not have imagined including a chapter on antisemitism in a book about Israel education. I must also acknowledge, right or wrong, that even as I sit here devastated after the murderous atrocity committed on the first night of Hanukkah 2025 on Bondi Beach in Sydney, thatI remain a glass-half-full kind of person on this issue. I still believe that most people, the very silent majority, are good at heart despite the current dramatic rise in antisemitism.

Even so, Jewish educators must pay critical attention to the rise of Islamic fundamentalism in the world. Not to instill fear in our youth but because, among other crucial lessons, October 7 taught us that we must explain to them that not all people share the Jewish people's belief that all people are created *b'tselem Elohim* (in the divine image).[71] Our young people should know that, for some people in the world, extremism and violence are acceptable means of achieving brutal ends. By definition of terrorism instils fear in the masses, and we as a community must adapt to a reality whereby we are vigilant concerning such threats, while never allowing them to paralyze or define us.

My detractors will accuse me of having learned nothing from history. But I take this somewhat optimistic view partly because, it is engrained in me to always avoid succumbing to our enemies and also because I believe very strongly that Jewish identity must be built from within and not defined by external forces.

Antisemitism is our enemies' attempt to control our destiny. In response, Jewish educators must take control over how we confront the world's oldest hatred.

* * *

The diverse reactions of the teenagers to the Pittsburgh shooting highlighted the generational shifts in how experiences of antisemitism are perceived and how the subject is being taught. Previous generations of Jews experienced the Holocaust, knew a world without Israel, and sense the precariousness of Israel's existence. This is not the case for younger Jews today. Despite various threats and attacks they only know and can only conceive of a world with a strong Jewish community and an ever-present and powerful State of Israel.

We must also remember that Jewish communities around the world are not monolithic on these issues or indeed any issues. In the weeks and months after October 7, many of these divides were on full display, especially, but not only, in the responses from Jews with origins in the former Soviet Union, of Mizrahi descent, and especially from many Israelis living abroad.[72] When we talk about antisemitism, we must understand that not everyone comes to the discussion with the same lived experience.

As in all things, language and definitions are extremely important in education. There are many strong reasons to affirm definitions of critical terms that could be considered universal truths. However, it is my opinion, that when terms like "antisemitism" are disputed, or at least under discussion, it is not the best approach to simply tell learners, "I know some people don't agree with this definition, but this is the one we are going to use. Now let's move on."

In some instances, it might be useful to agree to a *stipulative decision*[73] in order to advance a conversation, rather than get caught up in a discussion of semantics. But in other moments, it is incumbent on the educator to decipher various definitions, at the very least to better understand why there is not universal consensus on contested terminology.

Many Jewish communal organizations have understandably insisted on the adoption of the International Holocaust Remembrance Alliance (IHRA) definition of antisemitism:

> Antisemitism is a certain perception of Jews, which may be expressed as hatred toward Jews. Rhetorical and physical manifestations of antisemitism are directed toward Jewish or non-Jewish individuals and/or their property, toward Jewish community institutions and religious facilities.[74]

One educational approach is to accept that this is the definition the community considers acceptable, so all young people should accept it as well. However, in the context of this book, and what is considered to be good education, even if that is the case, educators should still closely examine some of the eleven examples from the IHRA definition, focusing on those that specifically relate to Israel[75]:

1. Accusing Jewish citizens of being more loyal to Israel, or to the alleged priorities of Jews worldwide, than to the interests of their own nations.

2. Denying the Jewish people their right to self-determination —e.g., claiming that the existence of the State of Israel is a racist endeavor.
3. Applying double standards to Israel by requiring behavior not expected or demanded of any other democratic nation.
4. Using symbols and images associated with classic antisemitism (e.g., blood libel, claims of Jews killing Jesus) to characterize Israel or Israelis.
5. Drawing comparisons of contemporary Israeli policy to that of the Nazis.
6. Holding Jews collectively responsible for actions of the State of Israel.

Good Israel education demands this deeper exploration; for example, of clauses like "manifestations might include the targeting of the State of Israel, conceived as a Jewish collectivity."

As much as I detest our adversaries' incessant conflation of anti-Israel and anti-Jewish ideologies, we must acknowledge that the interconnectedness of Jewish identity with Israel, as I have argued earlier, can bring murkiness to this discourse—including through the IHRA definition.

The direct linkage of antisemitism to policies and actions of the State of Israel and, for some, the unqualified use of terms like "antisemitism," "anti-Israel," and "anti-Zionism" as essentially interchangeable, is something Jewish educators must explore with their learners.

For example, one could compare the IHRA definition to the Jerusalem Declaration on Antisemitism (JDA), released in 2021 and signed by scholars of antisemitism, Holocaust studies, and Jewish studies.[76] In it, antisemitism is defined as discrimination, prejudice, hostility, or violence against Jews as Jews or

Jewish institutions as Jewish. The JDA also makes it clear that not all anti-Zionism is antisemitism, marking a subtle difference from the IHRA definition, which goes out of its way to claim the opposite.

This discussion is not to be seen as any endorsement or rejection of a definition. But, to simply ignore the fact that aspects of the IHRA definition are controversial can come from two motives. One is somewhat commendable: The attempt to shield students from misinformation. But it can also be viewed as a form of negligent Israel education that attempts to manipulate students' viewpoints by shielding them from them such dissent.

For some, it might seem surprising that the debate over definitions can become so animated and contentious. Yet it continues to draw heated attention in certain communal and educational circles. The tension over these two approaches can be frustrating for educators working for organizations or institutions with strong opinions on these matters that demand adherence to a specific definition of antisemitism. However, teaching the contradiction between various definitions is good educational practice and ought to be supported by Jewish stakeholders. If the controversy is not taught, young Jews may well encounter it for the first time in a hostile setting, which is a far greater threat to their understanding of antisemitism. While some will argue that such distinctions are beyond the grasp of many of our learners, the underlying differences between definitions like these relate to other issues that, at the very least, Jewish educators should be familiar with.

It is also crucial for Jewish educators to acknowledge and clarify to their students that the three terms "antisemitism," "anti-Israel," and "anti-Zionism" have distinct meanings and interpretations, none of which are universally accepted. Below, I present my own preferred definitions, though I am well aware of the fact that some readers may disagree with them or argue that, even when multiple definitions exist, certain definitions should be prioritized:

- "Antisemitism" is a certain perception of Jews, which may be expressed as hatred toward Jews.[77]
- "Anti-Israel" is "extreme and/or illegitimate criticism of Israel," which may include false accusations against or delegitimizing the Jewish nation and does not include legitimate policy criticism.
- "Anti-Zionism" is a prejudice against the Jewish movement for self-determination and the right of the Jewish people to a homeland in the State of Israel.[78]

These distinctions are important, even though there is much evidence to suggest that, when acted upon, both anti-Israel and anti-Zionist ideologies are often blatant manifestations of antisemitism. But, in my experience, simply telling students that all anti-Israel or anti-Zionist sentiments are antisemitic "just because they are" is not adequate for the learner or the educator.

The stakes for the Jewish community are not minor. A few years ago, I appeared on a panel where I stated that, linguistically speaking, anti-Zionism was not always antisemitism. Within forty-eight hours, a funder chastised me and threatened to withdraw their donations if I did not retract my statement. To their credit, upon clarification the funding was not withdrawn. Moreover, for the record, I do believe that, in most cases today, anti-Zionism is almost always thinly-veiled antisemitism.

Slogans like "Free Palestine," "From the River to the Sea," and "Globalize the Intifada" are dangerous and often have severe and tragic consequences.[79] As an Australian, I feel this now more than ever due to the attack on Bondi Beach. After two years of unchecked protests, vitriol, and continued verbal and physical threats and assaults against Jews and the Jewish community, many are correctly suggesting that "words do matter," and that they have disastrous consequences.

Jewish educators must teach their learners about these slogans and their implicit threats. Although not a popular opinion in many corners of the Jewish community, I have come to recognize, that not all of those chanting these slogans fully understand that them as categorical calls to conquer all of Israel and annihilate all Jews. I offer this neither as a defense nor an excuse for these protestors.

While I accept that some will consider me hopelessly naïve, I believe that not all those who use the slogans above fully understand how they are internalized by many Israelis and Jews.[80] My message to educators is that their role, before judging and condemning the motivations of the chanters, is to first and foremost teach their learners how and why these slogans are problematic, and that many are both anti-Zionist and antisemitic.[81]

Educators must teach their learners that words matter. The old childhood chant that "sticks and stones might break my bones, but words will never hurt me" is inadequate and untrue. While it is not my place to dissect the distinction between organized, coordinated, and lone wolf antisemitic attacks, it is our collective responsibility as educators to ensure that all people understand the power of rhetoric and slogans when heard by certain individuals who then decide to act on them in violent ways.

Educators must recognize that learners encounter slogans like these on social media, in pop culture, from their peers, and even from politicians. So, Jewish educators must be prepared to teach their learners about the origins of these slogans, the various contexts in which they appear, and the motivations behind them. I think this is a better approach than merely telling learners that these slogans are vitriolic statements that should be categorically dismissed without consideration.

This type of education is difficult, because it requires us to understand populations that may despise us. But we do ourselves a disservice if we cannot do so.

All of this is important because good Israel education must expose learners to diverse viewpoints even when they are challenging and uncomfortable, even on some of the most distressing topics of our time—antisemitism foremost among them. Understanding this broader context will ultimately empower our learners to better confront antisemitism.

* * *

The purpose of Jewish education is not to eradicate antisemitism. It is to enable young Jews to identify antisemitism and stand up against it, educate people about it, and minimize its reach and impact.

I believe that a critical starting point for Jewish educators is the "3 Ds" of antisemitism as initially articulated by Israeli human rights advocate and politician Natan Sharansky. The "3 Ds" stand for "delegitimization, demonization, and double standards."[82]

> Delegitimization: Denying Israel's right to exist as a Jewish state while allowing other states premised on ethno-nationalism [or whichever term you prefer] to exist.
>
> Demonization: Portraying Israel or Jews as inherently evil or malicious through hateful or exaggerated rhetoric.

> Double standards: Applying unfair or uniquely harsh criticism or expectations to Israel that are not applied to other countries.

Even with these three categories, I've observed that many Jewish educators, often unfamiliar with the history of antisemitism, struggle to recognize when antisemitism infiltrates discussions about Israel. Consequently, I've chosen two classic antisemitic tropes and provided examples of how they manifest in Israel-related conversations. This is not an exhaustive curriculum, but highlights the importance of Jewish historical knowledge for today's Israel educators.

The Protocols of the Elders of Zion

The *Protocols of the Elders of Zion* is an antisemitic text apparently composed by the Tsarist secret police in the early twentieth century that falsely claims to reveal a Jewish plot for global domination.

In accordance with the *Protocols*, references to Israel trying to take over the world have been used in various settings to argue against the Jewish state's right to exist. Some of these settings include television shows in the Arab world,[83] textbooks used by the Palestinian Authority,[84] Iranian political discourse, far-right[85] and far-left conspiracy theories,[86] the 1998 Hamas Charter,[87] and on social media platforms where terms like "globalists" and "puppet masters" are thinly veiled references to the tropes of the *Protocols*.

Newspaper cartoons have sometimes garnered much attention for these depictions including the now infamous cartoon that appeared in the *New York Times* that depicted Israeli Prime Minister Benjamin Netanyahu as a dog leading a blind President Donald Trump, who wears a kippa[88]

A more recent example is a cartoon featured in Australia's *The Sydney Morning Herald* and *The Age* on January 7, 2026, implying that Israeli Prime Minister Benjamin Netanyahu is behind calls for a Royal Commission on antisemitism only a few weeks after the murderous attacks on Bondi Beach.[89]

Another prominent manifestation of this is the long-running and frequent allegation that pro-Israel lobbying organizations like American Israel Public Affairs Committee (AIPAC) use monetary donations and political lobbying to control or heavily influence US lawmakers, effectively coercing them into supporting Israeli government policies,[90] a trope that also finds its way into many antisemitic conspiracy theories.

The Blood Libel

The *blood libel*, which originated in the Middle Ages, is the false and fantastical antisemitic accusation that Jews murder non-Jewish children to use their blood for religious rituals. This myth has fueled violence and persecution for centuries.

Perhaps one of the most striking recent examples of the blood libel trope is the accusation that Israel has deliberately targeted babies as part of its military strategy.[91] These claims are self-evidently false, and the tragic cases in which children have died in the current war have taken place unintentionally, due to Hamas' use of hospitals and other civilian sites as terrorist strongholds. Even many of the charges of unintentional collateral damage have later been debunked by credible impartial sources.

The claims that the IDF is deliberately targeting Gazan babies is a modern manifestation of the blood libel charge. Political theater stunts that involve actors consuming raw meat, drinking blood, and using Israeli flags as napkins is a form of the blood libel as well. It extends to claims that Israel is pursuing a genocidal policy against the Palestinians. Acknowledging this does not dismiss the fact that it is a tragedy when innocent lives are lost in war.

* * *

As educators, we all make choices. I could walk into a class and tell students that such-and-such is antisemitism, and this is how they should respond to it. Especially in today's climate, I understand the attraction of such an approach. It allows no room for uncertainty and sets clear expectations for both the educator and the learner.

I often give a presentation entitled, "The Inherent Contradictions of Youth Today." In it, I explain that my research has found that teenagers can sustain cognitive dissonances that adults cannot. For example, young people are skeptical of authority, but are often willing to follow social media influencers without question. They see the world as complex but also adhere to certain binaries such as "oppressor vs. oppressed." My favorite example is that young people today tend to be narcissists who also want to save the world.

This kind of cognitive dissonance is important for Jewish educators to understand, because when it comes to Israel education, they are ever present. For example, I once showed a teenager the *New York Times* cartoon referenced above and they said to me, "I can see why it's antisemitic, but it's also kinda funny too."

One significant difference between the perceptions of young Jews and some older Jews is that, despite the rise in antisemitism in the US, many young Jews still believe they live in the freest country in the world and don't think the world is "out to get them."

No matter how many times people tell them about swastikas painted on bathroom stalls, Jews attacked while out for a leisurely walk, and even shootings in synagogues, many young Jews today do not feel that their lives are under immediate threat. As the "lockdown generation," they repeatedly tell us that they are more scared of going to our schools than to our shuls.

Even though the data indicates otherwise, Jewish teens have also repeatedly told me that the suggestion that Jews are persecuted more than other minorities is wrong and they resent being told otherwise.

They are deeply affected by the historical suffering of the Jewish people and feel a profound connection to Judaism's unique history, culture, and traditions. However, they view our history as a call to action. They think we must stand up and ensure that "Never Again" means "never again" for us or any other human being. Today's Jewish youth are proud Jews who see no contradiction between embracing their Jewish identity *and* their commitment to humanity and making the world a better place.[92]

This is all especially challenging for Jewish educators because much of today's antisemitism occurs online, which is an environment in which many of our learners are more experienced than we are. Moving forward, Jewish educators must become more knowledgeable about the internet, social media, and artificial intelligence to effectively support their learners.

Overall, we must also remember that the role of the Jewish educator is different from that of organizations focused on combating antisemitism. In the context of Israel education, the task is to empower learners to recognize antisemitism and how it is used to demonize Israel and the Jewish people. If, as a result of this education, an individual decides to pursue an advocacy path, either by defending Israel or fighting antisemitism, that is laudable, but such pathways can never be equated with the good Jewish and Israel education that should precede it.

* * *

It can be scary to be a Jew in the world today. Each day, the news is filled with stories of attacks on Jews. Sometimes they are clearly antisemitic and sometimes they are connected to what is taking place in Israel. Often, they are both. These distinctions are worthy of discussion for educators.

When such incidents are connected to Israel and the Middle East conflict, the immediate response could and probably should be that Jews around the world should not be held accountable for Israeli actions. However, I have myself argued that all Jewish identities are and should be based on some relationship with Israel: land, people, nation, and state. It is true that attempting to make a nuanced argument on the distinction between antisemitic and anti-Israel incidents is not a viable strategy. However, ignoring or dismissing the distinction in educational settings is not either.

If our educational goal is to strengthen the Jewish connection to Israel, we must acknowledge that a sense of responsibility for what Israel does is almost unavoidable for some individuals. As educators, we must find ways to help learners understand and defend the distinction between antisemitism and anti-Israel ideologies when necessary. Ignoring this issue would be a mistake, because we cannot avoid the fact that while Jewish education promotes a positive connection with Israel, much of the world hurls this relationship back in our faces.

* * *

Considering all this, it's undoubtedly crucial for Jewish educators to think about how to prepare and empower their students to confront antisemitism.

In general, when confronted with antisemitism Jews have several options. The first is to ignore the incident. Sometimes, a response will inflame a situation or have negative aftereffects. This must be taken into consideration.

I understand this may not be a popular choice for many readers but consider the perspective of a young person who simply wants to live peacefully without causing trouble. As their educator, the question is not whether you would have made the same decision, but how you can support your learner who has chosen this path.

Another option is for a person to respond immediately. If you are an educator responsible for learners who might be inclined to retaliate against antisemitism, your task is to prepare them to identify antisemitism and equip them with the information and skills necessary to respond appropriately.

A third option is to refrain from responding to an antisemitic incident immediately but to address it at a later stage. For example, if a student encounters antisemitism in the classroom or on school grounds, they might decide to report the incident to an authority figure to help manage the situation. This approach could lead to more strategic and possibly more effective responses, such as writing formal letters, organizing petitions, or staging demonstrations.

These options are intended to remind readers that educators should never rely on a single approach to combat all forms of antisemitism. I present them because Jewish educators must provide learners with alternatives that suit their needs, rather than urging them to do what others expect them to do.

Our learners live in complex communities they must navigate every day. It is rarely in their best interests for an outside organization to decide on the best solution for the challenges these young people face. Of course, young people should receive support and resources when appropriate. However, as a community, we must also trust them to navigate the environments they inhabit.

* * *

I recognize the personal fears of Jews at this time. However, incorporating these anxieties into classrooms, youth groups, and summer camps is not an effective educational approach in the short or long term. Jewish educators must avoid instilling in learners the belief that a healthy Jewish identity can be developed on the basis that others despise us.

Jewish educators should let students know that they are aware of and concerned about rising antisemitism. However, it is important not to leave them with the impression that their world is overwhelmingly violent and hostile. This will only paralyze them. True growth requires both an understanding of the threats they face and the knowledge and skills needed to navigate and overcome difficult times.

All of this is challenging in an environment in which one of the most common questions Jewish educators worldwide face is: "Why does everyone hate us?" This feels even more painful because many Jews of all ages report that their "friends" and "allies" have been silent, less than empathetic, and sometimes openly hostile since October 7.[93]

But to be a Jewish educator today means leaning into the question of "why everyone hates us," because it is an opportunity to help young people unpack all the emotions and challenges that it raises. Many of us would feel much more comfortable citing the words of Fred Rogers: "Look for the helpers. You will always find people who are helping." However, the reality is that we can't always shield our children from the surge of antisemitic incidents worldwide.

Perhaps the task of the educator is not answer to the question "Why does everyone hate us?" Instead, it might be to ask more questions: "What makes you ask this?" "Did you experience hate?" Have others told you they feel this way?" Educators must be skilled enough to identify the emotions—perhaps confusion or fear—that trigger this question and others.

Questions to Consider

- How do you make the distinction, or not, between anti-Israel sentiments, anti-Zionism, and antisemitism?
- If someone were to ask you, "Why does everyone hate us?" how would you respond?

6

Evolving Divisions, Boundaries, and Conversations

My wife and I are in a WhatsApp group with five other couples. One of them is an Israeli couple who spent time living in the US.

The thread began as a social outlet, but after October 7 it focused on issues related to Israel. We wanted to support our Israeli friends, but we also shared information and debated various issues. There was considerable diversity of opinion but most of the time the discussions were civil.

However, one day a group member referred to a Jewish political figure with whom they disagreed as a *kapo*. Let's just say I lost it. "At the point where one of our good friends is calling a fellow Jew a *kapo*, a line has been crossed," I said. "I can't stay in a group where this type of language goes unchecked."

The word "*kapo*" is one of the most offensive slurs a Jew can hurl at another Jew. It refers to Jewish prisoners the Nazis forced to supervise other Jews in ghettos and concentration camps.

Some *kapos* attempted to alleviate the suffering of their fellow Jews, while others inflicted brutal beatings, participated in selections for death, and enforced Nazi orders in return for minor privileges or survival.

In today's context, whether intended or not, the term implies that someone is a lesser Jew, possibly not even a Jew at all. More insidiously, it charges that they are actively working to harm other Jews.

Some Jews, usually on the Right, have used terms such as "self-hating" or "self-loathing" to describe Jews they believe are harming the Jewish people. On the Left, terms like "fascist," "extremist," "racist," or even "Nazi" are used to discredit fellow Jews.

Natan Sharansky and Gil Troy have revived the derogatory term "Un-Jew" to refer to Jews who remain Jewish but reject, abandon, or seek to undo what Sharansky and Troy consider fundamental components of modern Jewish identity—specifically, a Zionist understanding of Jewish peoplehood and connection to the State of Israel.[94]

Some have pointed out to me that incidents like the sinking of the Altalena[95] and the incitement leading up to the assassination of Yitzhak Rabin prove that this is not a new phenomenon. Jews have long been vitriolic toward one another. But the concept of Jewish peoplehood is important and sacred to me. As such, I believe that all behavior and language designed to alienate or excommunicate a fellow Jew is unacceptable.

There is empirical data that personal interactions have been stretched and strained since October 7. One study reported that 64 percent of Jews felt that discourse around the Israel-Hamas war affected their relationships, 53 percent avoided discussion, and 12 percent had ended a friendship or relationship after the other person expressed antisemitic views.[96]

This discord extends to the Jewish family. I thought that writing a family Haggadah for Passover 2024 was challenging but 2025 was even more difficult.

By April 2025 the war against Hamas had been going on for eighteen months, hundreds of Israeli soldiers had been killed, many thousands of Palestinians were dead, and there were still close to sixty hostages being held in Gaza.

Our seder guests were an eclectic group gathered in Memphis, Tennessee. They were both Jews and non-Jews, ranging in age from twelve to eighty-five. There were some with strong Jewish backgrounds and others with almost none at all. What we all had in common was curiosity and a willingness to learn. Most importantly, the group came prepared to have a good time.

Despite the desire for a "good time," how could we not mention what was taking place in Israel and Gaza? How could we construct a Haggadah that made the Passover story relevant and meaningful to everyone at the table without referring to it? More important, would we be able to hold conversations at the table that didn't deteriorate into argument and disturb what was meant to be a celebration?

Tensions always exist within families, but they have increased since October 7, especially but not exclusively between generations.[97] Recently, I learned about an attempt by a mother and daughter, Rabbi Amy Eilberg and Penina Eilberg-Schwartz, to open a dialogue by writing letters to one another about their feelings related to Israel and Gaza, and then to share their correspondence publicly.[98] An article about this relationship stated, "When we reach out across our painful divides and build bridges to those we disagree with, we are insisting, again, that no person is disposable."[99]

I later learned that the person from our WhatsApp group who used the word "*kapo*" did not intend it in the way I understood.

Nor did it have the same connotations for them, or others in the group. Perhaps I overreacted, but still, this did not lessen the pain I felt that a fellow Jew would use such a word against one of our own.

This experience reminded me that Jews today often face complicated—even hostile—situations in their personal, professional, and communal lives. As challenging as it is in those moments, individuals can choose to walk away or, in some cases, be asked to leave situations and environments that lead to confrontation, even within their own families.

Good Jewish and Israel education should neither push people away nor ask them to leave. If only it were that easy.

* * *

At its best, Jewish education should strive to be inclusive, tolerant, and respectful, creating a space for a diversity of voices. However, in order to do this, institutions must develop strategies to honor all individuals and their worldviews.

Even with these strategies, some individuals may choose to leave if their differences cannot be resolved. Others might be asked to leave if they are not a good fit. However, this does not lessen the responsibility of Jewish and Israel education to strive to serve everyone who chooses to participate.

Organizations with a specific ideological focus may find it easy to create a list of activities that align with their viewpoint. However, I encourage these institutions to consider including diverse perspectives. At the very least, engaging with "the other" can help solidify existing ideas and beliefs, and it can expand people's perspectives and understanding. This creates more opportunities for engagement.

Organizations that prioritize pluralism and diversity always face challenges in managing different opinions. Common approaches include hosting panels that showcase multiple perspectives, creating source sheets with varied texts, and inviting speakers with opposing viewpoints. However, even these activities must follow clear principles. Frequently, the voices and sources that are left out are just as significant, if not more so, than those included. Above all, such activities must be conducted in a way that encourages participants to challenge the ideas presented, rather than the individuals expressing them.

Since October 7, these practices have been challenged in all Jewish institutions. *Ad hominem* attacks on individuals, in real and virtual spaces, seem to be more widespread than ever before. The line between what is acceptable and what is not has shifted. Even concepts such as "Left" and "Right" now mean different things. Much of what seemed banal has taken on enormous emotive significance.

One of the biggest challenges for Jewish and Israel education in a post-October 7 world is how to maintain firm positions on Israel while fostering inclusive education. How can we achieve this when certain viewpoints challenge or contradict these positions?

* * *

"Rabbi Abahu said: The main tent of our
patriarch Abraham was open on both sides."
(Bereshit Rabbah 48:9)[100]

In educational settings, it is essential to establish clear guidelines for which voices can be included or excluded. Although educators often lead these challenging discussions, all stakeholders in the institution must agree on the rules. Once these guidelines are set, the educator is responsible for creating practices and pedagogies that allow multiple voices to engage with one another within that framework. In some cases, the educator can co-develop these parameters with learners. However, in every case, the educator must design the learning framework based on sound educational principles, free from undue external influence.

This is easier said than done. Since October 7, many educators have told me that they know what to do for their learners, but their bosses, lay leadership, or funders won't allow them to do it. This illustrates the tension in Israel education between inclusive pedagogy and limits on deviant viewpoints. As shown in Dr. Keren Fraiman's research on barriers in Israel education, it is essential that all necessary stakeholders consent to those limits.[101]

"What emerged from my research speaking with educators from across North America…is that they all experienced one ultimate barrier to teaching about Israel and 'the conflict': a lack of institutional and communal support," Fraiman wrote.[102] She goes on to discuss how educators can only be at their best if they have full backing and support from institutional leadership.

Educators often face competing forces that dictate what is permissible and intolerable in their practice. Some factors are beyond their control, making it difficult, if not impossible, to navigate.

One issue is whether the learner is participating voluntarily or if they have the agency to leave a given environment. Educators generally strive to create welcoming and inclusive conditions for all learners. However, as many educators have experienced, even the most pluralistic environment can be challenged. When the stakes are high, the outcomes may not always align with expectations.

A few decades ago, I taught an Israel studies course to a class of fifteen-year-olds at a Jewish day school. I tried to lay down ground rules for robust discussion and disagreement.

I told the learners, "This course is designed to challenge all our thoughts and opinions about Israel. I want to encourage all of us to be open and honest as well as respectful and empathetic to all viewpoints expressed. But this class is not just about Israel, it's also about civility and community. So, let's say from the outset that hate speech, racism, and calls for violence won't be accepted in this class." I added, "If it's acceptable in the Knesset, then it's pretty much acceptable in this classroom."

I thought I was being very clear and transparent: Everyone's opinions were to be respected and valued, but there were still clear boundaries. I even explained why these boundaries existed.

But one student stated his belief that all Arabs were guilty of crimes against Jews and therefore legitimate subjects of any military action whatsoever.

As a novice teacher, I repudiated the student's remarks, which left him feeling alienated and ostracized. Today, if faced with the same situation, I would respond differently. I would aim to be more tolerant of the student and his viewpoints. I would do so not because I condone racism or violence in my classroom, nor because similar sentiments are sometimes expressed in the Knesset, but because a classroom must always prioritize creating a safe and respectful environment for all students.

* * *

Paradoxically, creating safe and respectful environments requires strong, explicit parameters. I value the diversity of the Jewish people and believe all good education should include diverse viewpoints, so I offer three criteria for such parameters: Boundaries, Safety, and Challenge.

1. All Educational Settings Need Boundaries

Setting boundaries is one issue on which Israel education must become proactive rather than reactive. Time and again, educators have learned the hard way that it is far more difficult to enforce boundaries only after they have been crossed.

To give a few examples from an article in *In These Times*, "There is the Hebrew education director in New England who says she was fired after singing about a ceasefire. The volunteer coordinator at a Baltimore County synagogue who was let go shortly after they were seen at a demonstration. The Sunday school teacher in Illinois who says they were dismissed after showing students a video of a Palestinian comedian. A veteran camp counselor who says she was harshly interrogated over a social media post—and then not invited back to a job she held for years."

This a serious problem. The same article states, beginning with reports of educators wearing keffiyehs to Hebrew school, at least 20% of one religious school's, "staff departed, either fired or resigned, with several saying they were pushed out—in the roughly nine-month period after October 7."[103] If the educators involved had known what their institutions' boundaries were from the beginning, perhaps their removals would not have come as a surprise.

It is true that many of these issues surfaced or were magnified very suddenly due to October 7. Many Jewish institutions were taken by surprise. Today, however, there is no excuse for failing to create and articulate clear boundaries for educational discourse. Indeed, every community and organization has such boundaries, whether they admit it or not.

It is not sufficient for an individual teacher and their supervisor to agree on these boundaries. They must be embraced at every level of leadership within the institution and clearly communicated to all stakeholders. This ensures that teachers or camp counselors receive support from their principals or camp directors, and that parents—or age-appropriate learners—can actively assess whether the institution meets their expectations. Choice in Jewish education is essential, but equally important is the institution's commitment to transparency.

I often hear about problems that arose not because there were no boundaries established, but because people did not know what they were. As Shuki Taylor, *chief executive officer of M²: The Institute for Experiential Jewish Education,* states:

> One of the biggest challenges in Israel education right now is ambiguity. Educators and leaders are afraid—afraid of being fired, of upsetting parents or boards, of saying the wrong thing. With no clear institutional lines, they're left paralyzed. Additionally, even when lines aren't the issue, many have internalized the idea that holding nuance means never stating clear convictions. We've confused complexity with relativism. Institutions need a process—whether a survey, facilitated conversation, or coaching model—to define what's in bounds and what's not. Educators need help building the muscle to articulate what they believe in, even in the face of disagreement. We can hold nuance and still stand for something. But we need to teach people how.[104]

2. Safe and Brave Spaces

When I taught *hadracha*[105] courses, I was often asked about how long ice breakers should take in a group setting. I would let them know that the purpose of ice breakers is to make people get to know each other and feel comfortable around one another. Therefore, ice breakers should go on for as long as it takes. Similarly, creating safe spaces in education should not be bound by a predetermined amount of time.

A safe space in education is an environment where students feel emotionally, physically, and psychologically secure to express themselves without fear of ridicule, discrimination, or harm.[106] Classrooms, especially those that incorporate sensitive and marginalized identities and experiences, must foster environments of mutual respect.[107]

In Jewish educational settings, educators have often addressed complex topics by creating safe environments. Recently, educators like Dr. Rachel Fish have been vocal in advocating for a shift from safe spaces to "brave" spaces, particularly regarding Israel.

> Start today by engaging with individuals with whom you can: create brave spaces which are needed to foster and cultivate communities of people who desire to engage with differences; engage with people who believe and value the dignity of all human life irrespective of ethnic, religious, and national identities; and invest time with individuals who are willing to engage with complexity without seeking the demise of any particular community.[108]

The idea of choosing "brave spaces" over "safe spaces" emphasizes that inclusion is only the starting point. True learning—especially on challenging or sensitive topics—requires a level of productive discomfort, rather than emotional insulation.

Creating a brave space means setting clear norms that promote respectful dialogue, active listening, and thoughtful risk-taking. It recognizes diverse perspectives and existing power dynamics. Instructors contribute by modeling vulnerability, sharing their own learning experiences, and encouraging students to critically examine assumptions and voice differing opinions. Structured discussions, ongoing reflection, and constructive conflict management support this process. Continuous feedback ensures the classroom can adapt to its evolving dynamics.[109]

One of the significant challenges posed by this approach is the quality of educator it requires. The educator who can create brave spaces in Israel education must not just be confident in their knowledge of Israel but also have tremendous pedagogic skills and the ability to manage difficult, challenging, and confrontational viewpoints. At the same time, they must maintain harmony in a diverse and inclusive educational setting.

3. Challenge in Jewish and Israel Education

In 2011, my teacher Dr. Joseph Reimer and I discussed the critical concept of "challenge."

As experiential educators, we felt that Jewish educators should aim to encourage participants to undertake the challenge of progressing toward more complex participation in Jewish life. Because there is a lot more to Judaism than participating in a Jewish camp or youth movement, experiential educators need to motivate individuals to move beyond their comfort zone and creatively explore a variety of Jewish modes of expression.

In our view, it was not enough for experiential Jewish education to provide the "Jewish air" for participants to breathe. That is a fine goal for Jewish socialization. But engaged Jewish youth will grow into the creative leaders of tomorrow's Jewish community only if they learn to deal with complexity and risk.

We agreed that experiential Jewish education is uniquely positioned to promote learning from challenge. Whether they are struggling with how to alleviate world hunger or bridge the gaps between diverse Jewish populations, engaged youth need to experience their Judaism as a serious arena for generating substantive responses to the deepest challenges their generation will face.[110]

This concept of "challenge" was largely developed from the work of University of Chicago Professor Mihaly Csikszentmihalyi and his concept of "flow." Flow is described as a psychological state characterized by complete immersion and focused engagement in an activity.

In a state of flow, people often lose track of time, experience intense enjoyment, and perform at their best. Examples include an athlete in the "zone" or a musician fully immersed in their performance. Flow occurs under specific conditions: clear goals, a balance between challenge and skill, immediate feedback, and autotelic motivation (engaging in the activity for its own sake).[111]

To achieve a true sense of flow in education, the learning experience must be challenging. Unfortunately, Israel education is often criticized as being overly simplistic or even pediatric. Activities such as bringing a camel to school, picking oranges to showcase Israeli agriculture, or making an ice cream cake in the shape of Israel can serve as engaging introductions. However, these are too frequently treated as the primary or peak experience of Israel education, rather than stepping stones to deeper learning.

Educators often know when their learners are in a state of flow. I've certainly witnessed it in an experiential framework when children are involved in an outdoor activity like a ropes course or white-water rafting.[112] But I have also witnessed it when learners are deeply engrossed in a discussion, a commemoration, or listening to a great speaker. It only ever happens when the learners are being challenged. For the educator, the moment when nothing other than the educational process matters for the learners should be cherished and repeated.

* * *

Today, Israel education is often viewed as divisive in many educational environments. It needs to evolve into a practice that unites people with different perspectives, encourages them to engage in dialogue and debate, and bridge divides within the Jewish community.

Jewish education has always embraced argument and a diversity of opinions. Israel education should be no different. Two classic Jewish texts and the Jewish pedagogies derived from them are models for the future of Israel education: "*eilu v'eilu*" (these and those) and "*machloket le'shem shamayim*" (an argument in the name of heaven).

Eilu v'Eilu (These and Those)
Talmudic Passage (Eruvin 13b:10–11)

רַבִּי אַבָּא אָמַר שֶׁשָּׁלֹשׁ שָׁנִים נֶחְלְקוּ בֵּית שַׁמַּאי וּבֵית הִלֵּל:
הַלָּלוּ אוֹמְרִים הֲלָכָה כְּמוֹתֵנוּ וְאֵלּוּ אוֹמְרִים הֲלָכָה כְּמוֹתֵנוּ.
וְיָצְאָה בַּת-קוֹל וְאָמְרָה אֵלּוּ וְאֵלּוּ דִּבְרֵי אֱ-לֹהִים חַיִּים הֵן,
וַהֲלָכָה כְּבֵית הִלֵּל: וְכִי מֵאַחַר שֶׁאֵלּוּ וְאֵלּוּ דִּבְרֵי אֱ-לֹהִים
חַיִּים הֵן, מַדּוּעַ זָכוּ בֵּית הִלֵּל לְהַקְפִּיד לְהָקִים הֲלָכָה כְּמוֹתָם?
— שֶׁהָיוּ נוֹחִין וַעֲלוּבִין, וּמְשַׁנִּין אֶת דִּבְרֵיהֶם וְאֶת דִּבְרֵי בֵּית
שַׁמַּאי; וְלֹא רַק זֶה, שֶׁמַּקְדִּימִין דִּבְרֵי בֵּית שַׁמַּאי לְדִבְרֵיהֶם...

> Said R. Abba in the name of Samuel: Three years the school of Shammai and the school of Hillel disputed. One school said that the Halakhas prevail according to their opinion, p. 28 and the other claimed that their decrees should stand. Finally a heavenly voice was heard to the effect that *both schools [eilu v'eilu] disputed as to the words of the living God, but the Halakhas prevail according to the school of Hillel.* Now if it be true that both schools dispute as to the words of the living God, why should the school of Hillel be thus favored? Because the members of the school of Hillel were modest and patient, and would always repeat the words of the school of Shammai. Not alone this; but they also always gave the school of Shammai precedence when citing their teachings.[113]

Like Beit Hillel, Jewish educators should present alternate views with humility and dignity, fostering practices that encourage authentic learning. Diverse opinions allow learners to choose their own path, knowing their choices are valued and respected.

Machloket Le Shem Shamayim (Argument in the Name of Heaven)

Pirkei Avot 5:17

> כָּל מַחֲלוֹקֶת שֶׁהִיא לְשֵׁם שָׁמַיִם סוֹפָהּ לְהִתְקַיֵּם,
> וְשֶׁאֵינָהּ לְשֵׁם שָׁמַיִם — אֵין סוֹפָהּ לְהִתְקַיֵּם

> "*Every controversy that is in the Name of Heaven shall in the end lead to a permanent result, but every controversy that is not in the Name of Heaven shall not lead to a permanent result.*"[114]

In integrating debate into the educational setting, the guiding principle should be that of an "argument in the name of heaven." This means the goal is not to convince others to adopt a specific point of view. Instead, the purpose of engaging in such discussions is to consider all perspectives before solidifying one's own beliefs. Adopting this approach is essential to ensure that Israel education is thoughtful and reflective rather than dogmatic. Embracing constructive disagreement, with its clear pedagogical benefits, is critical to achieving this aim.[115]

This carries with it a few important assumptions. The first is a pedagogic one: Such discussions and debates should only be introduced to learners when it is developmentally appropriate. However, research indicates that younger children are generally more capable of understanding nuance and complexity than educators might imagine.[116]

Another assumption is that not every class or program about Israel must be filled with complexity and disagreement. There are moments when just learning to appreciate Israel are appropriate and should be encouraged.

Other assumptions have to do with Israel itself. Israel is not a perfect country. While this may seem obvious, it has not always been reflected in Israel education. Many educators are so determined to get their learners to love Israel that they present the country as perfect. This does not reflect the Israeli reality, which is as complex and flawed as any other.

Finally, we must assume that good education requires learners to be exposed to the truth. They must be given multiple perspectives on all critical topics. They must be afforded the opportunity to develop their own beliefs, values, and opinions.

Presenting viewpoints opposed to the traditional Zionist narrative is not designed to tear that narrative down, but to strengthen it. Learners who are presented with alternative viewpoints will hold their own opinions with greater conviction, even if those opinions differ from those of their teacher. This will become even more crucial when learners encounter less favorable perspectives on Israel in external and sometimes hostile settings.

I remember the first time I personally experienced racism in Israeli society. It wasn't during my twelve years in Jewish day school or during my education in the Labor Zionist youth movement. Those were the places where I learned that Israel celebrates Jewish immigration from around the world, which is something that continues to inspire me. It was only when I walked through Afula for the first time, meeting Jews from the former Soviet Union and local residents, that I began to understand what some have said: Israel loves immigration but often hates immigrants.

So began my own personal journey to better understand not just the contemporary makeup of Israeli society but the sordid history of a country that still needs to grapple with issues like the Yemenite Children Affair (*Ma'aseh Te'eymanim*)[117] and the Ethiopian AIDS scandal,[118] as well as broader issues like racism in sports, the treatment of Israeli Bedouins, and high crime rates in Israeli-Arab communities. This learning journey endures as I continue to admire and be in awe of a country that boasts a diverse population, with Arab and Jewish doctors working together in hospitals and Arab members serving in the Knesset.

Although the claim repulses me, let's explore the implications of applying these two principles to one of the most pressing questions facing Jewish youth and young adults today: Is Israel committing genocide in Gaza?

A Jewish educator or institution might choose to ignore the question entirely because they strongly disagree with its premise. They believe that even addressing it would lend it undeserved credibility. While this approach reflects a clear ideological commitment, the question is not going away. Most Jews will encounter it in some form whether in school, at university, in the workplace, or among their peers.

For many years, Jewish educators have been encouraged to teach their learners about "Purity of Arms,"[119] a foundational ethical principle of the IDF. It is offered as proof that the Israeli army is the "most moral army in the world." Often, this is supplemented by biblical and Talmudic sources. Such lessons tend to conclude with remarks like, "Even with the best of intentions, mistakes and accidents occur in all wars."

However, images of the recent war in Gaza are constantly livestreamed into the phones of our youth along with the perpetual claim that the IDF is not only immoral, but committing genocide.

So, the Jewish educator has a choice to make. They can rely only on Israeli-sanctioned proof texts to elicit a certain response, or they can introduce learners to a multiplicity of viewpoints. They can do so in the safe space of a Jewish setting before learners hear about them from confrontational or antagonistic external sources.

This issue is being discussed in the media, on social media, and in high school and university classrooms around the world. Your learners are being exposed to it no matter what you do. This means that you cannot pretend it does not exist, and you must discuss it in a Jewish educational setting.

The Jewish educational framework should be expanded to include texts and sources that define terms like "genocide." These texts should actively discuss the morality of war and include voices that both accept and reject the premise that Israel's actions in Gaza might be considered genocide. Jewish educators should prioritize including the perspectives of Israeli soldiers in these discussions, especially those who risked or sacrificed their lives. These soldiers were striving to protect innocent lives while targeting the real enemy.

Educators' fear of this approach is valid. What if a student emerges from the discussion disagreeing with the educator? What if the student starts to believe that the IDF is not always acting in the most ethical manner? What if the student concludes that Israel is committing genocide? Alternatively, what occurs if a student challenges their progressive teacher by asserting that Israel's moral standards are exemplary and that the civilian casualties in Gaza are significantly lower than in other urban conflicts?

The fear is valid, but so are the risks of failing to engage with such issues. For example, if an educator simply says the genocide accusation is blatantly false, antisemitic, and a modern-day version of the blood libel, students may well agree.

In other cases, learners will be more skeptical of such an aggressive approach. They may feel they are being indoctrinated. As a result, their trust in the educator begins to dissipate. In the end, they may even turn their backs on the educator and indeed the Jewish community. Thus, a less nuanced approach to this issue can backfire badly.

I want to remind Jewish educators that *this* is the worst-case scenario. The worst-case scenario is not that a learner leaves an educational experience with an opinion that differs from yours or your organization. The worst-case scenario is that learners cease to trust us and walk away from us and perhaps the Jewish community as a whole.

As divisions continue to grow both within the Jewish community and in the wider world, Jewish educators have a vital responsibility: to raise a generation capable of engaging with differing opinions in constructive and meaningful ways "in the name of heaven." Doing so will not only make the learning experience deeper and more authentic but will also plant the seeds for a future world that is more inclusive, diverse, and filled with proud Jews of many backgrounds.

In a subsequent chapter we will explore further the boundaries and limits of appropriate voices to include within Israel education. The key question that continues to plague me as a Jewish educator is, at what point does exposing learners to certain voices run the risk of being interpreted by learners as endorsing such convictions?

The recency of the horrors of October 7 makes it difficult to suggest that hardline Palestinian narratives, and certainly not the perspectives of Hamas terrorists, should be included in Israel education. And even with that being said, I have been exposed to many highly acclaimed Holocaust and civil rights curricula that respectively include the narrative voices of Nazis and the Ku Klux Klan (KKK), certainly not to elevate these views, but to give students an insight into how such horrors were made possible. I am however skeptical that it is only the distance of time that was the criteria for such decision making.

However, in the very real discussion for educators about which voices to include, citing extremist examples is a distraction from the core educational issue at play—the limits of viewpoint diversity in education. Fundamentally the issues of including diverse viewpoints is not about which of our enemy's voices should be included within Israel education, but rather what the limits are of Jewish (and other) perspectives that should be incorporated in such discourse.

For many people there are views held by Jews that are considered extreme and beyond the pale of inclusion, and certainly beyond endorsing or platforming, within Jewish institutions. Here I can point to examples from both poles of the political spectrum, from the self-labeled anti-Zionists to hardline Israeli ultranationalists, which have been declared as unacceptable within certain sectors of the Jewish community.

For Jewish educators the criteria for engaging with even the most challenging and controversial, ideas must differ from those in the broader Jewish world. Educators presenting such perspectives is not an endorsement of "extreme" views, but an act of courageous education—one that prepares students to navigate the full complexity of the world they inhabit, especially when it challenges their deepest beliefs. The fear by some that learners will adopt extreme viewpoints because educators expose them to those ideas is understandable but not well-founded—as in today's world people will be confronted by those ideas regardless. Not without struggle, this approach, allowing learners to encounter multiple, diverse, and even extreme viewpoints first in a safe space, ensures that they are not left feeling surprised or deceived if they encounter them later in more hostile or antagonistic environments.

Questions to Consider

- When have you changed your opinion on an issue of substance as a result of being exposed to a challenging viewpoint?
- What are the boundaries beyond which you can no longer engage in dialogue with someone?

SECTION 3
Recharging Israel Education

הישן יתחדש, והחדש יקודש

(Ha-yeshan yitchadesh, ve-ha-chadash yikudash)
"The old shall be renewed, and the new shall be made holy."[120]

The Hebrew language uses various forms of the verb שדחתהל (l'hitchadesh), "renewal," to describe things like recharging one's phone, but also renewing oneself.

Especially after October 7, Israel education requires renewal and recharging, or at least an interrogation. We are, after all, living in a new reality.

This section of the book deals with five crucial areas of Israel education that must be "recharged." It explores the divide between particularists and universalists; the evolving nature of Jewish peoplehood and Zionism; reorienting *hasbara* (Israel advocacy); fostering a renewed emphasis on listening and empathy; and committing to joy and pride as the ultimate goals of Jewish and Israel education.

Only when these five areas are recharged can Israel education meet the changing reality of the post-October 7 world. What all five have in common is that they will require educators to understand that their role is not to be the fountain of all knowledge, thought, and belief. Instead, they must be providers of educational experiences that allow learners to experience their own journeys, even if they reach conclusions different from their own.

Janusz Korczak was director of the Orphan's Home in the Warsaw Ghetto during World War II. He maintained the dignity of the children as best he could until he, his colleagues, and the orphans were deported to the Treblinka extermination camp in 1942 and murdered.

Many people know about Janusz Korczak's final years, but fewer know of his life before the war. He was an educator, pediatrician, advocate for children's rights, and, to my mind, a thinker who brilliantly articulated what good education should always be.

He wrote:

> Children are not the people of tomorrow, but people today. They are entitled to be taken seriously. They have a right to be treated by adults with tenderness and respect, as equals. They should be allowed to grow into whoever they were meant to be. The unknown person inside each of them is the hope for the future.[121]

7

Recharging the "Vav" in the Particularism and Universalism Divide

הוּא הָיָה אוֹמֵר, אִם אֵין אֲנִי לִי, מִי לִי. וּכְשֶׁאֲנִי
לְעַצְמִי, מָה אֲנִי. וְאִם לֹא עַכְשָׁיו, אֵימָתַי

[Rabbi Hillel] would say, "If I am not for myself, who is for me? If I am for myself, what am I? And if not now, when?"
Pirkei Avot 1:14[122]

In February 2024, The Jewish Education Project, together with several partners including The iCenter and The Jewish Agency, began sending delegations of educators to Israel. These Mishlachot Areyvut (Delegations of Responsibility) bore witness to the events and aftermath of October 7.

In one session, the Hillel quote above was taught to the group by Rabbi Abi Dauber Sterne from For the Sake of Argument (FSA). The location was a Tel Aviv hotel that was then home to hundreds of evacuees from a kibbutz in the Gaza envelope.[123]

The underlying message of Abi's presentation—which took place only a few months after October 7—was that many Jews abroad, especially progressive Jews, who had spent a great deal of their energy focusing on "If I am only for myself," now needed to focus on "If I am not for myself."

The session revealed an underlying tension, but it failed to fully capture the extent of the anxiety that this dissonance has caused many Jews in the aftermath of October 7.

Initially, attention was directed at progressive Jews who had long supported their allies through difficult times but now found themselves isolated, abandoned, and silenced by those same friends. Notable examples included women's groups refusing to condemn the sexual violence that occurred on October 7, progressive groups excluding pro-Israel organizations, and minority racial groups, particularly those traditionally supported by Jews, turning against their Zionist and even Jewish supporters.

Shortly after the war in Gaza began, many other Jews, who were steadfastly committed to the safety and security of the Jewish people, also faced intense scrutiny. Accusations of myopic tribalism hindered their ability to acknowledge, let alone empathize with, the suffering of innocent Palestinians during the war.

Such a divide is certainly not new. I grew up with traditional Jewish liturgy, and I remember the dissonance I felt the first time I heard *kol yoshvei tevel* (all who dwell on earth) included in the *kaddish* prayer by progressive Jews. I was accustomed to the traditional version of the prayer, which speaks only of bringing peace to all the people of Israel.

This divide has become particularly intense since October 7. Much of the controversy has focused on the two poles of Rabbi Hillel's statement. It has been acknowledged that there are indeed two camps of Jews. Broadly speaking, there are the particularists, whose core orientation is "if I am not for myself."

They think almost solely in terms of the welfare and survival of the Jewish people. Then there are the universalists, who feel that they cannot be only "for myself." They are dedicated to ensuring that Jewish values serve as a beacon for the entire world.

* * *

Labeling these distinct groups as universalists and particularists is both reductive and inadequate. But this does not diminish the perception—and perhaps the reality—that since October 7, Jews seem to be drifting even further apart from each other on the basis of these categories.

Ezra Klein, a *New York Times* opinion columnist and podcast host, highlighted this divide in a very public manner. He used these broad categorizations to describe the deep divisions among Jews over the New York City Democratic mayoral primary, which saw a decisive victory for the staunchly anti-Israel Muslim socialist candidate Zohran Mamdani, who later won the general election:

> Many older Jews I know are shocked and scared by Mamdani's victory. Israel, to them, is the world's only reliable refuge for the Jewish people. They see opposition to Israel as a cloak for antisemitism. They believe that if the United States abandons Israel, then Israel will, sooner or later, cease to exist. To them, Mamdani is a harbinger. If he can win in New York City—a city with more Jews than any save Tel Aviv—then nowhere is safe.
>
> Many younger Jews I know voted for Mamdani. They are not afraid of him. What they fear is a

> future in which Israel is an apartheid state ruling over ruins in Gaza and Bantustans in the West Bank. They fear what that means for anti-Jewish violence all over the world. They fear what that will do—what it has already done—to the meaning of Jewishness. Their commitment to the basic ideals of liberalism is stronger than their commitment to what Israel has become.[124]

This division is not just over labels. Sometimes it involves harsh criticism.

The term "Tikkun Olam Jew" is sometimes used disparagingly to describe universalists, implying they focus on global suffering and oppression while neglecting the interests of their fellow Jews. Conversely, terms like "ethno-nationalist" or "racist" are sometimes used to criticize particularistic Jews, suggesting that their focus on the Jewish people comes at the expense of all other human beings.

Since October 7, these criticisms have become even more intense. "Tikkun Olam Jews" are accused of self-hatred or self-loathing by some, especially since Jewish progressives were abandoned by their allies after the horrors of October 7. On the other side, particularistic Jews have been increasingly accused of promoting ethnic supremacism, often using the words of right-wing Israeli ministers like Itamar BenGvir[125] and Bezalel Smotrich[126] as evidence.

Understanding this context is crucial for Jewish and Israel educators because many Jewish educational settings are connected to institutions, organizations, or movements that are firmly identified, or perceived to be identified, with one of the two camps. For Israel education to be effective, the distinctions between these two types of Jews must be understood, and the divisions between them must be mitigated.

This brings us back to Hillel's quote. To me, the most important Hebrew letter in the quote is "vav," meaning "and." The quote is often used to draw a distinction between two types of Jews, but the "vav" in the original *combines* the two—the particular and the universal. It states that they must exist in tandem. Jewish education should follow Hillel's dictum and empower our learners to be both universalist and particularist Jews.

* * *

In the weeks following October 7, I attended a powerful synagogue service at the Reform Congregation Beth Elohim in Brooklyn. In her sermon, Rabbi Timoner, who might be considered a universalist by certain standards, recounted how Noam Tibon, a retired major-general and father of *Haaretz* writer Amir Tibon, drove from Tel Aviv to Nahal Oz to rescue his son, daughter-in-law, and two granddaughters, who were trapped in their safe room surrounded by Hamas terrorists.

Rabbi Timoner noted that Noam Tibon did not save everyone he encountered on his way to his family, and emphasized, "No one would say that Noam Tibon was wrong for choosing to save his family before other people's families."

The reason, she said, is that, "We live in concentric circles of love, in concentric circles of care, in concentric circles of obligation. And that is okay, it is human, it is right. It is good to care first and most about those closest to you, and then outward in widening circles, and it is okay to prioritize our own group's grief before we focus on the grief of others. It is right to rise to save our own people before rising to save others."[127]

A crucial message for Jewish educators dedicated to the holistic development of their students' identities is that we live within these concentric circles, rather than at opposing poles.

It should not be controversial for a Jewish educator to teach our young people both that October 7 was the deadliest day in Jewish history since the Holocaust *and* that there are innocent people dying in Gaza. Yet it is. But these two facts do not contradict each other. Educators who seek to downplay one or the other are often manipulating their learners due to the educators' own ideological commitments.

I urge readers not to interpret these statements as attempts to draw comparisons or establish any moral or military equivalence between the various sides of the Israeli-Palestinian conflict. Without drawing any such parallels, I must continue to insist that in all good Israel education there must be context that draws upon multiple facts, various opinions, and differently held truths.

In the end, our people need to learn the Jewish teaching, "Kol Yisrael areivim zeh la-zeh"—"All of Israel is responsible for one another."[128] They also need to learn that Israel should strive to be an "Or LaGoyim"—"a light unto the nations."[129] They must be presented as intertwined, not contradictory.

In this regard, I have been influenced by Jonny Ariel, founding director of Makom: The Israel Education Lab at The Jewish Agency for Israel. He wrote about the need for a "cosmopolitan approach" to Israel education.

Cosmopolitanism entails viewing oneself as a part of a larger, interconnected world, transcending the confines of a single national, ethnic, or cultural identity. In Israel education, a cosmopolitan approach fosters learners' comprehension of Israel within a global framework, encourages the consideration of diverse perspectives (including Israeli, Palestinian, and global Jewish viewpoints), and promotes ethical reflection on learners' role as Jews in the wider world.

Importantly, Ariel suggests that students can deeply value and connect to both Israel (patriotism) and the wider world (cosmopolitanism) by pairing cosmopolitan with patriotism. This allows them to cultivate awareness, empathy, and ethical reasoning about both themselves and the world.[130]

Since October 7, many of these issues have become even more complicated and heated. There are times when this cannot be overcome. In some cases, learners may become familiar with and empathetic to alternate perspectives. In others, universalists and particularists may find themselves unable to see eye to eye.

Nevertheless, it is crucial for educators to address these dilemmas: Should Jews primarily focus on combating antisemitism, or should we maintain a strong commitment to fighting all forms of racism and hatred? Should Jews urge Israel to provide more humanitarian aid to Gaza? Should there have been an immediate ceasefire to end Palestinian suffering or was Israel right to continue the war until it felt its security was safeguarded and all living hostages were released?

One approach could be for an educator to offer their opinion on these and other controversial issues. Most of the time, I am dismissive of this approach, though it does have its virtues. Nonetheless, on some issues there is a clear and certain "right and wrong" and thus a need for absolute moral clarity. Each educator and their institution must decide what those issues are and be transparent about them.

Most of the time, a far better approach is to present each of these issues as vastly more complicated than they initially appear. Good education demands that educators present multiple opinions and viewpoints on these issues, and allow learners to reach their own conclusions.

Educators often fear the second approach because they worry that students might choose the "wrong" position on these issues. I believe that by embracing Hillel's "vav," this fear is mitigated. The educator can allow learners to believe "a little bit of this and a little bit of that." For example, they can permit learners to conclude that it is possible to be both pro-Israel and pro-Palestinian rights, which many young people today believe.

This approach does not seek to downplay the real challenge of such divisions. Families and communities have been literally torn apart by them. For a family unable to sit at the same table for a Passover seder, a Hebrew school that fires all its educators for wearing keffiyehs to class, or a Jewish philanthropic organization that decides to provide financial aid to Palestinians, it is overly simplistic for me to suggest that all they need to do is consider two opposing truths.

I acknowledge this challenge, but I sincerely believe that Jewish education is not the place to "resolve" these issues. It should be a space in which learners can explore all possibilities as they develop their belief systems on such important matters.

However, Jewish education also plays a crucial role in shaping the Jewish community we want to see. Although there were initial signs of unity in the months following October 7, the Jewish community is currently fractured. The divide between particularist and universalist Jews is one of the most significant fault lines. Healing is necessary, and this process can and must begin with Jewish education.

* * *

For me, there was no issue that symbolized the need for Jewish educators to renew Hillel's "vav" than that of redeeming the hostages. While our Jewish brothers and sisters were in captivity, the Jewish people were not whole. It was hard even to imagine moving forward as a people until the hostages, alive and dead, were returned.

Pidyon shvuyim, "redeeming captives," is a Jewish commandment that, many have argued, overrides all others.

פדיון שבויים קודם לפרנסת עניים ולכסותן
ואין מצוה גדולה כפדיון שבויים

"Redemption of captives comes before aiding
and clothing the poor and there is no *mitzvah*
greater than the redemption of captives."
Shulchan Aruch, Yoreh De'ah 252:1[131]

In the context of the debate between the particular and the universal, it could be asked: Does it matter that not all of the hostages were Jewish or even Israeli?[132]

Here, I offer two different perspectives that, I believe, do not contradict each other.

The first is one that I articulated in an article entitled, "Redeeming the hostages is the Jewish educational imperative of our lifetime":

> We must continue to wear yellow ribbons and "Bring Them Home" dog tags. At all of our events, we must continue to have an empty yellow chair and conclude by singing "*Acheinu*." We must continue to hear the voices of the hostage families and raise our own voices to all politicians. Eventually, we will stop counting the days since Oct. 7, but until then, we must continue to count every single day. Educators can transmit information, teach texts, raise complex questions, look at historical events from multiple

> perspectives and much more; but sometimes educators must simply teach through example and model certain moral imperatives of maintaining the constant awareness and presence of those in captivity.
>
> As Jewish educators, we must continue to stress that the freedom of the hostages is a human issue and not just a Jewish issue (we can also remind learners that several of the captives are themselves not Jewish). We must also impart to our children that they are not just living through historic times, but that they are a part of creating the memory of this time for generations to come.[133]

An alternative perspective to my view that redeeming the hostages represents the greatest Jewish peoplehood moment in our lifetime can be found in the words of two remarkable individuals, Rachel Goldberg-Polin and Jon Goldberg, the parents of the murdered hostage Hersh Goldberg-Polin.

In their speech at the Democratic National Convention in August 2024, Rachel and Jon addressed an audience filled with people of many faiths and nationalities: Christians, Jews, Muslims, Hindus, and Buddhists from 23 countries. In the speech, Rachel affirmed: "In our Jewish tradition, we say *kol adam olam um lo'o, every person is an entire universe. We must save all these universes."* She urged immediate action to bring home *all* 109 hostages then in Gaza.[134]

Rachel went on to tell the following story:

> One thing gave me a whisper of hope on October 7, because one of the witnesses with whom I

> spoke told me that when the rocket fire began and when all those hippies went running into the bomb shelter, there was a Bedouin man who was a guard at the kibbutz across the street and he ran into that same shelter and as Hamas closed in on the bomb shelter, the man said, "Stay quiet, let me go talk to them" and went outside and said in Arabic, "I am a Muslim. Everyone inside is my family. They are Muslim. You don't have to search in there." He tried to save them. He could have said, "I am a Muslim" and just saved himself, but he tried to do the right thing even though it was terrifying and even though it required unimaginable courage. He was brutally beaten and the witnesses do not know what his fate was, but I take comfort for a fleeting moment that there was someone trying to do the right thing when everything in the universe had been turned upside down. We human beings have been blessed with the gifts of intellect, creativity, insight, and perception. Why are we not using them to solve global conflicts all over the world? Because doing this is hard and takes fortitude and imagination, grit, risk, and hope. So instead, we opt for hatred because hatred is so comfortable and so very, very easy.[135]

From the beginning, Rachel and Jon were vocal about their unwavering commitment to rescuing all the hostages. They repeatedly emphasized that there were non-Jewish and non-Israeli hostages who also needed to be saved.

While some may argue over whether the rescue of hostages from Gaza was a Jewish issue or a universal one, the distinction was unnecessary. It should have been clear from the beginning that it was both.

* * *

Regardless of whether one believes we are in an evolutionary or revolutionary moment in Israel education, or whether the issues discussed in this section are of longstanding or arose only after October 7, Jewish educators must adapt immediately. As Jonny Ariel wrote, "When Israel, Jewish identity, and education are each in a state of profound flux, Israel education for Jews will necessarily be dynamic."[136]

Over the weeks and months since I initially wrote this chapter, some trusted colleagues have asked me a simple question: Is it really enough to just bring back Hillel's "vav"? My answer is that, while I firmly believe that the future of Jewish education, Israel education, and the Jewish people may depend on this "vav," I am also increasingly convinced that prioritizing the particular, followed by the universal, is crucial.

While Jewish people must continue striving to make the world a better place, this commitment must also stem from a strong sense of Jewish identity and community. I frequently hear, particularly from Jewish day schools, that fostering Jewish identity and providing students with a strong sense of self better prepares them to engage with and embrace diversity after graduation.

This approach is also grounded in various Jewish sources, which state that one must take care of one's family and community before assisting others. Based on Talmudic sources, many Jewish educators have used the "lifeboat" analogy to express this concept. They note that, if you're adrift at sea, you must first ensure your own survival before you can help others.[137] Recently, many Jewish educators have adopted the "airplane" analogy, emphasizing that passengers are always instructed to use their own emergency oxygen masks before helping children or others.

Good educational practice does not require choosing between the universal and the particular. It involves fostering a strong sense of self that influences broader commitments. These are foundational concepts of positive psychology introduced to me by my mentor, Jonathan Woocher. Positive psychology holds that developing one's own strengths and well-being is not selfish. In fact, it is essential to meaningful social contribution. Confidence, resilience, and a clear sense of purpose enable individuals to act effectively and sustainably for others.

By investing in personal growth, individuals enhance their ability to lead, inspire, and make a tangible difference, creating a ripple effect beyond themselves. Thus, self-cultivation is inseparable from social impact. The more fully one develops their potential, the greater one's ability to improve the world around them.[138]

In a world dominated by binaries, it is crucial to reclaim the "vav" that links the particular and universal aspects of being Jewish. Equally important is recognizing that self-knowledge is the most solid foundation for Jewish education. Strong Jewish learning empowers individuals to be outstanding contributors to the Jewish community, which in turn equips them with an unwavering commitment to improving the world.

Questions to Consider

- What are some moments in your life when you have felt the need to put your particular interests ahead of your broader concerns?

- When in your life has this tension between universal and particular concerns been challenged and even deviated from its usual course?

Recharging Jewish Peoplehood and Zionist Education

In 1990, after finishing high school, I spent a year living in Israel. The first half of the year was spent at the Machon Le Madrichei Chutz La'Aretz[139] and the second half on Kibbutz Yizre'el near Afula in the north of Israel. Coincidentally, my parents were volunteers on this kibbutz during the 1967 Six-Day War.

On the kibbutz, there was a Garin Nahal,[140] a group of Israelis more or less the same age as me and my fellow volunteers. By and large, they looked just like us, including guys with lots of long hair.

For much of our five months on the kibbutz, we did almost everything together with our Israeli contemporaries: working in the fields and factories, eating in the communal dining room, and partying in the kibbutz pub. We felt at one with them, until we didn't.

I remember the precise moment we all realized how different we were from them. One Friday evening, we Aussies (and Kiwis) turned up to the kibbutz pub at the regular opening time and found the doors locked. About an hour later, our Israeli friends invited us inside. We were stunned by what we saw.

The room was dark. The normal music had been replaced with somber Hebrew songs. There were lots of tears. The girls were standing, holding some sort of machines in their hands. We later learned they were electric shears from the sheep shed. The men were now completely bald and piles of hair lay on the floor of the pub.

It was a ceremony to mark the weekend before the Israelis enlisted in the Israel Defense Forces. Soon, they would leave to become soldiers and perhaps risk their lives. As for us, we'd remain on the kibbutz harvesting almonds and working in the amaryllis fields.

This experience taught me that, even for the most committed amongst us, there are always explicit and implicit divides between Israelis and Jews from around the world. Celebrating the similarities and confronting the differences have always been a major focus of Israel education. At the same time, it has been recognized that the State of Israel today is a culmination of millennia of the Jewish people's history. For Israel education to thrive, it must be grounded in a strong sense of this peoplehood.

Over the past two years, one of Israel education's more challenging tasks has been talking about a post-October 7 world, because many Israelis are still very much in an October 7 mindset.

I was recently reminded of this as I planned to meet an Israeli colleague at a conference. Unfortunately, she had to cancel her trip because her husband has been called up for reserve duty yet again. This brought the number of days he had been on active service since October 7 to over 300.

Even though the last living hostages have returned from Gaza and a tentative ceasefire is in place, Israel still seems to be at war on multiple fronts. Additionally, the country is grappling with the challenges of PTSD, ongoing trauma, and internal divisions that sometimes threaten to tear the fabric of Israeli society apart.

In contrast, Jews living outside of Israel are largely operating with a post-October 7 mindset. Despite the increase in antisemitic incidents, they are actively working to build and strengthen communities for the future, rather than dwelling excessively on the past. Thus, notwithstanding the initial surge of unity between Israelis and Jews worldwide following October 7, the differences between these two groups seem to be growing.

A primary objective of Israel education should be to promote learning, understanding, and empathy regarding the experiences of Israelis and Jews living outside Israel. To achieve this, educators should avoid portraying these communities as monolithic entities. Instead, they should promote learning that acknowledges Israelis and Jews worldwide are as diverse as the seventy faces of the Torah.

* * *

"Distancing" between Israelis and Jews worldwide is not new. In the early 2000s, several research studies led to the emergence of a "distancing theory" that posits that Jews around the world, especially younger, liberal, and American Jews, are becoming increasingly emotionally and ideologically distant from the State of Israel.[141] Even though this theory was controversial and contested, many policies were put in place to try to bridge the divide.[142]

Building strong relationships between Israelis and Jews worldwide is essential to fostering positive ties between these two distinct communities. Relationship building, in the deepest sense, is a proven method of ensuring that Jews feel a strong sense of connection with their fellow Jews and, specifically, the people of Israel. Similarly, Israelis need more opportunities to understand Jewish life outside of Israel.

However, to build these relationships and bridge these divides, we must acknowledge the genuine gaps that exist and, in some cases, how wide they really are. While I firmly believe that Jewish educators can recount moments of profound connection to Israel, I am equally confident that they can also share instances of feeling distanced or even alienated from Israel and its people.

I can relate many personal anecdotes that illustrate this distancing, and just as many that show how deep and enduring the impact of encounters with Israelis have been on my life. I believe anyone involved in Jewish and Israel education has similar stories.

For example, in the summer of 1995, I led a group of Jewish Australian college leaders on a trip to Israel. We were fortunate enough to be granted an audience with then-President of Israel Ezer Weizman[143] at his residence. After a pretty standard "Israel cheerleader" type of presentation, there was a brief silence among the hundred or so students present.

I don't particularly enjoy silence, so I raised my hand to ask what I thought was an innocuous question. I don't even remember what it was, but it began something like this: "Mr. President...," which Weizman may have heard as "As my president..." It didn't matter, because Weizman immediately interrupted me in his well-known loud and booming voice: "How dare you call me your president! Come and live here. Then, and only then, can you call me your president!"

I sheepishly sat down. No one dared ask another question.

Today, President of Israel Isaac Herzog would never utter such a statement. His long commitment to and respect for global

Jewry extends well beyond his days as Director of The Jewish Agency. He is an Israeli who sees Jewish communities around the world as more than just the philanthropic arm of the State of Israel. I feel honored to be among the inaugural council members of his visionary initiative, the Voice of the People.[144]

Yet many Israelis' disdain for Jews living outside of Israel is genuine. Israelis often still adhere to the concept of *shlilat ha'golah*, or the negation of the Diaspora. They are certain that Jewish life outside Israel will eventually end due to antisemitism or assimilation. They cite the Golden Age of Spanish Jewry followed by the Expulsion and the Inquisition, and the grandeur of German Jewry followed by the Holocaust, as historical proof.

When Israelis see increased antisemitism in the world, they often see Israel as the only viable path for Jewish life. Even before the state he envisioned was founded, Theodor Herzl wrote that, due to the nature of antisemitism, the only solution was the creation of a Jewish state.[145]

For many Jews living outside of Israel, such thinking is considered naïve and arrogant given the vibrant Jewish lives they live. Even with increased antisemitism around the world since October 7, it remains unclear how Jews around the world will respond in both thought and action.

Many Israelis, on a personal and often visceral level, believe that Jews living outside of Israel lack the same "skin in the game" when it comes to Israeli security, politics, or society—and they might be right.

Once, during a college program I led in Israel, I sat next to a bus driver on a long night drive. We agreed to talk throughout the drive, both to help him maintain focus and help me improve my Hebrew. He got to know me a bit, and was eager to discuss what he saw as my misguided liberal political views and persuade me that "Bibi was king."

I informed the driver that I was open to discussing any topic he wanted. However, I cautioned him that, if he argued that my perspective was invalid because neither I nor my children would be compelled to serve and risk our lives in the Israeli army, we would have to end the discussion. This was not because I lacked the ability to respond. It was because he would be right. I knew that I would feel immense guilt and have no suitable response to him or to myself.

This gap in understanding and experience is one of the key reasons that, for the last seven years, I have regularly facilitated conversations with Israeli educators about Jewish life in North America.

I often say things like: Let me to tell you a bit about myself and my family. My father's family came to Australia from Poland in the 1930s. As the saying goes, they saw the proverbial "writing on the wall" and made a good life for themselves in Australia. My mother was born in Foehrenwald, a displaced persons camp in Germany, in 1946. It was there that my maternal grandparents met.

My Buba was born in Riga, Latvia and was a survivor of ghettos and concentration camps. My Zaide, from the small Polish town of Zelechow, had fought with the Russian partisans. In the DP camp they were given a choice and, as family lore has it, they didn't have long to decide: "The United States, Palestine, or Australia?" They chose Australia, the furthest place they could imagine from the horrors of Nazi Europe.

I have recounted my family story dozens of times, often to audiences of Jews from numerous countries. I always conclude, "Now look at you and look at me. If not for a single decision, made in haste and in the most adverse of all circumstances, we could be sitting in each other's places." I add that I understand that mine is an Ashkenazi story, but a similar conversation could be had between Sephardi Jews from different parts of the world.

Recent encounters with Israelis during which I have shared this story proved to be extraordinary opportunities to discuss the intersections of Israeli identity and Jewish life in America. During one encounter, I shared a raft of statistics with Israeli educators:

- Approximately 80% of North American Jews are not Orthodox.[146]
- Over 70% of Jews vote Democrat.[147]
- 73% of non-Orthodox Jews are married to someone who is not Jewish.[148]

One of the Israeli educators basically did a "mic drop." "See," she said, "there is no future for Jews in the Diaspora."

I looked at her and said, "And 93% of Jews in America are proud to be Jewish."[149] I walked over to her, motioned for her to pick up the invisible "microphone" she had "dropped," and said, "You see, it isn't so simple...and it isn't all that bad."

Moreover, even after deliberately pushing a few Israeli buttons with comments like, "Israel makes life for Jews in America very difficult" and "Jews in the Diaspora should have a vote on certain issues in the Israeli parliament," the talk always ends in the same way: "So, what can Jews living in communities outside of Israel learn from you as Israelis, and what can you, as Israelis, learn from Jews living outside of Israel?" Then we hug and say *le'hitraot*, "see you later."

* * *

Since October 7, some Jewish educators have felt compelled to revise their language. Previously, they often used pithy truisms to describe the relationship between Israel and Jews worldwide. However, these statements now require serious examination.

Some examples include:

1. "Israel is a safe haven for all Jews."

   In many ways this statement is the foundation of modern Zionism. But after what occurred on October 7, no educator could suggest to their learners that all Jews are completely safe in Israel. Even with the strength of the Israeli army on one side and increased antisemitism outside Israel on the other, it is difficult to say to learners that Jews are categorically safer in Israel than elsewhere.
2. "Israel will always be there to bring Jews home, no matter what."

   For decades, Jewish educators have told their learners about the Aliyot from distressed lands in Europe, Ethiopia, the Middle East, North Africa, the former Soviet Union, and elsewhere, along with the rescue of Jewish hostages at Entebbe in 1976. They cite these examples as evidence that Israel will save Jews wherever they are. This statement was certainly a truth for me until my good friend and colleague Elliot Goldstein, a cousin of murdered hostage Hersh Goldberg-Polin, said, "As my son chooses what army unit to enlist in, I now have to tell him that I actually no longer believe that the Israeli government will do absolutely everything possible as an utmost priority to bring him home."

Dismissing these statements as mere language issues undermines their significance, as they sometimes signify breakdowns in key aspects of Israel and Zionist education. For most Israelis, particularly those with strong Zionist backgrounds and ties to the IDF, the idea that these statements are being questioned is often difficult and troubling. This was demonstrated after the return of the last (deceased) hostage Ran Givli in January 2026. Many strong Zionist voices claimed that this moment was evidence that Israel would always do whatever it could to return every Jew to their families. For Jews living outside Israel, failing to challenge these sentiments can be deeply troubling.

I've spoken to many Jewish educators who, when they had to make the necessary language changes, embarked on profound introspective journeys about their own beliefs regarding Israel. I admit that Eliot Goldstein's words still tear at my soul. Given the profound nature of statements like these, both in terms of language and core beliefs, it is no surprise that many Jewish educators have found themselves in conflict with many Israelis, both those residing in Israel and those living abroad. These statements could potentially represent a new reality in the relationship between Israel and global Jewry.

Amid the current events in Israel and Gaza, we are hearing contrasting stories from Jewish educators. Some are stepping away from Zionism, Israel, and even Judaism. They no longer want to feel complicit in the ongoing attacks on Gaza. In contrast, many other Jewish educators say they have never felt a stronger connection to Israel than they have since October 7. On a call with Jewish educators during the 12-Day War with Iran in 2025, more than one said something like, "I know that I actually couldn't do anything if I was in Israel now, but it's weird, there's no place I'd rather be than in a bomb shelter in Tel Aviv."

It's not simple to identify the specific emotions behind such deep connections. Sometimes it is love; at other times, guilt or even shame. But October 7 certainly exacerbated these feelings for many Jewish educators. To deal with it, many Jewish educators I know have made it a point to have at least one Israeli friend or colleague who has become their "eyes and ears on the ground." Someone to tell them what the real feeling is on the street. Someone to inform them that there has been another missile alert and they are running to a bomb shelter yet again in the middle of the night.

Bridging the divides between Israelis and global Jewry can and should happen on a personal level. However, in the post-October 7 reality, simply continuing the same efforts to connect people is not enough. Major, necessary paradigm shifts are required to bring these communities together. Central to these changes is the revitalization of both Jewish peoplehood education and Zionist education.

The connection between Jewish peoplehood and Zionism is strong, but they are not the same. Avishai Margalit argues that our shared past is the most meaningful bond for the Jewish people. He argues that Zionism is not the only expression of Jewish peoplehood, but rather the result of deep-seated moral commitment to build and maintain a nation-state, even as statehood raises complex tensions.[150]

However, while Jewish educators must play a central role in any efforts to reimagine Jewish peoplehood and Zionism, they should only be responsible and accountable for the educational aspects of these efforts. By allowing Jewish educators to concentrate on education, they will be freed from much of the communal discourse surrounding these sensitive issues and empowered to better serve their learners.

Reenergizing Jewish Peoplehood Education

Shlomi Ravid, a leader in the field of Jewish peoplehood education, stated that "peoplehood" has always been defined by "the consciousness of the shared sense of belonging to the Jewish people, past, present, and future. It is the framework that enables Jews—across differences of geography, belief, and practice—to see themselves as part of one collective story."[151]

I cite this definition because it goes beyond the usual Jewish peoplehood slogan "Am Echad, Lev Echad" (One People, One Heart).[152] Shlomi's definition focuses on the "past, present, and future" of the Jewish people, acknowledging that peoplehood is more than just a matter of thinking and belief, but also of "practice." It is what Jewish people *do* and *will do*.

Jewish peoplehood education has often relied on a passive approach, emphasizing the past and present while largely overlooking the future: the active behavioral outcomes necessary for its success. These approaches frequently, whether implicitly or explicitly, position Israel as the central focus of the Jewish peoplehood paradigm. I suggest that the role of Israel should be examined in a more nuanced way than traditional Jewish peoplehood and Zionist educational models have typically allowed.

The first approach to teaching this subject sees Israel as the locus of Jewish peoplehood. Many Jewish educators teach about different Jewish communities from around the world, and I distinctly remember learning and teaching, even at times dramatizing Jewish communities in Russia, Ethiopia, Morocco, Iran, and so on. Often, the "punchline" was that all of these communities have somehow found themselves in Israel today. In this context, Israeli Jews were never really discussed as a single Jewish community, but rather as the home for various *edot* (ethnic communities).

Such activities often sparked significant discussions on the nature of Israeli society. They frequently revolved around the question of whether Israel should be considered a "melting pot" or a "multicultural" society. Some educators used the "chocolate cake" as a metaphor for the melting pot. Each individual's distinct ethnic and cultural ingredients and flavors were brought together and integrated to create a single, delicious Israeli cake. On the other hand, a "garden salad" metaphor was used to represent multicultural Israel. Multicultural Israel brought together vegetables from all over the world to create an equally tasty salad, but each ingredient retained its own distinct flavor.

A second approach in Jewish peoplehood education emphasizes the similarities and differences between Jews globally, with a tendency to focus on similarities. Many Jewish learners participate in activities like placing colored pins on world maps to indicate where their grandparents, parents, and they themselves were born. This method often involves exploring commonalities in geographical origins, cultures, and religious practices among diverse groups of Jewish learners.

Then, the educator often asks the group where they would like their children to be born. This allows students to visualize that we are all one Jewish people and shifts the conversation to one about Jewish destiny.

While this activity may be age appropriate for certain learners, it largely overlooks or downplays the many tensions within Jewish peoplehood. These include not only the differences between Israelis and Jews living outside of Israel, but also the significant internal divides within Israeli society and within Jewish communities worldwide.

Pedagogical approaches like these are designed to educate learners about other Jewish communities worldwide and are essential for a comprehensive understanding of the Jewish people as a whole. As Rabbi Kook's triangle of identity discussed in a previous chapter points out, the concept of "Am Yisrael" is a crucial component of what it means to be Jewish in today's world.

Both approaches are deeply rooted in Zionist education. The first approach explicitly states that the Jewish people's exiled communities will eventually ingather in Israel. The second approach assumes that, in most Jewish learning groups, at least one person will have a connection to Israel, enabling the educator to highlight this aspect.

Jewish peoplehood education and Israel education are not the same, although they are often conflated. However, Jewish peoplehood education *is* critical to the future of Israel education; if for no other reason than that half of the world's Jewish population lives there.

Jewish learners should always learn about different types of Jews. This is important because understanding fellow Jews is essential to comprehending the broader Jewish community, and learning about "the other" often leads to self-reflection. Moreover, this is not only a way to unite Israelis and Jews from around the world; it should also be applied to global Jewry as a whole.

In addition to providing models of Jewish peoplehood education that enable Jews to learn about "other" Jews, I want to advocate for an additional layer of Jewish peoplehood education that goes beyond mere knowledge. This layer emphasizes experiencing other Jews and forging deep, authentic relationships with them. Let's call it Relational Jewish Peoplehood.

This pedagogic approach to implementing Jewish Peoplehood is not inherently new. However, my goal is to relieve Jewish educators of the responsibility and burden of uniting the entire Jewish collective. Relational Jewish Peoplehood recognizes that, when it comes to the global Jewish community, there are Jews with whom one can form deep connections and relationships, while others will remain simply "other Jews."

Relational Jewish Peoplehood recognizes that being Jewish is only one of many aspects that define Jewish individuals. Other values, dispositions, beliefs, and practices can be more prominent and may connect people even more than Jewish identity itself.

Unfortunately, this model is sometimes depicted as using crude generalizations and stereotypes. However, I believe that deeper relationships and even friendships are more likely to develop when socially progressive Jews from outside Israel connect with progressive Jews in Tel Aviv, and when modern Orthodox Jews from around the world connect with like-minded individuals in Efrat. In a more advanced approach, the organization Enter: The Jewish Peoplehood Alliance, through its One2One initiative, has created algorithms that connect Jews globally based on their hobbies and interests, such as sports, popular culture, and religious practices.[153]

Jewish educators should focus on building and nurturing relationships with like-minded Israelis and Jews globally. This strategy is crucial as it highlights that Israel encompasses more than just government policies and social media updates. It authentically reveals the diversity of Israelis, offering a connection point for Jews worldwide. Additionally, this approach relieves educators of the burden of addressing the challenges of the entire Jewish community, allowing them to make a meaningful and enduring impact specifically on their learners.

Of course, such an approach should not compromise programs and platforms that unite diverse Jewish individuals. Encouraging and expanding programs that bring together varied Jewish voices is crucial, as they play a vital role in shaping future Jewish leadership and fostering mindsets that can ultimately bridge the divide between Israelis and Jews.[154]

Successful Jewish peoplehood education often requires an element of action. As has been cited by many thoughtful Jewish educators, "Jewish peoplehood is not just this concept. It's actually a set of activities.... By doing something, you enact Jewish peoplehood."[155]

Today, action on Jewish peoplehood education must connect Jews globally, with a clear link to Israelis. Israel is or soon will be home to the largest Jewish population in the world and understanding this geographic and demographic fact is essential. Jewish peoplehood education must also take into account one of the most significant population changes in world Jewry today: The number of Israelis now living in Jewish communities around the world.

Naturally, such education should emphasize Israeli culture and the contemporary Hebrew language. It is true that there are other centers of Jewish culture and other Jewish languages, but neglecting Israel in this context is not merely an oversight. It is a failure to acknowledge and recognize some of the greatest Jewish achievements in history.

Reclaiming Zionist Education

Jewish education will always have a place for what could be called "traditional" Zionist education. These educational settings emphasize the Hebrew language, integrate Israel both implicitly and explicitly, and highly value Aliyah as an outcome. Youth movements, day schools, and summer camps are dedicated to these fundamental Zionist ideals and practices.

The proportion of young people involved in these traditional Zionist environments varies significantly around the world. For example, the United States has relatively low levels of affiliation with these types of organizations compared to communities in Australia, South Africa, England, France, and several South American countries. Zionist education is perceived quite differently across Jewish communities. While it is mainstream in some, it is increasingly marginal or countercultural in others.[156]

This may not be entirely bad. It could signify a resurgence of the original, countercultural ethos of the early Zionist movements. However, approaches that resonate within tightly knit Zionist circles may not speak to more diverse Jewish communities. Moreover, outspoken ideological messaging can alienate potential learners, particularly young people. This presents a classic educational dilemma: How to preserve traditional, ideologically driven models while simultaneously adapting them to broaden their reach.

I believe we need a renewed and adaptable form of Zionist education—one grounded in its fundamental principles but attuned to the present day—to make it relevant to a broader segment of the Jewish community. This is a mission shared by groups such as the Z3 Project.[157].

An analysis of traditional Zionist education worldwide is necessary. Although it is beyond the scope of this book, two significant trends can be identified. First, modern Orthodox Zionists dominate traditional Zionist life, irrespective of their proportion of the community. Second, there is a general decline in traditional Zionist education in most countries.

I firmly believe that, in light of current global dynamics, if we fail to develop a twenty-first century Zionist pedagogy that holds broader meaning and relevance, the term "Zionism" risks becoming a relic of the twentieth century. Many communities and educational institutions are already opting to use "pro-Israel" to describe their relationship with the Jewish state. The term "Zionism" is contested today, and if we wish to preserve its significance in the twenty-first century and beyond, Jewish educators worldwide must take significant responsibility for reclaiming the term.

For many young Jews today, Zionism is frequently defined by others. But as Zack Bodner, leader of the Z3 Project, says, "Some would abandon 'Zionism' as too polarizing, but the word is too important to lose. Changing our own language to suit our critics is not the right answer."[158]

Zionism is increasingly being characterized by anti-Israel and often antisemitic groups as an oppressive, colonialist, and genocidal ideology and regime. Jewish educators have a responsibility to challenge and refute these definitions. But we must also acknowledge that it has become the prevailing narrative about Jewish nationalism, frequently accepted and internalized by young Jews.

Zionism is also being defined by another force that alienates most Jewish youth outside Israel, especially in the US, and particularly among those who do not identify as Orthodox. Jewish educators must acknowledge and respond to it.[159]

Put simply, the characteristics of Zionism espoused by the current Israeli government and amplified in mainstream media and social media channels are antithetical to the values of most young Jews outside Israel, who are generally universalist and socially progressive. When progressive Jewish youth outside of Israel hear nationalist Israelis, including senior government officials, using violent and even racist language to describe their adversaries, it is no surprise that those committed to universalism and equality distance themselves from what they perceive to be the dominant Zionist narrative.

While I don't condone telling people how to label themselves, I've noticed a significant distinction between Jews who identify as anti-Zionists and those who are simply non-Zionists. For those actively working to dismantle Israel, I'm comfortable labeling them as antisemites, especially if Israel is the only country they see as a target for eradication. However, I've encountered many Jewish non-Zionists who would feel right at home at a protest rally in Tel Aviv on any given Saturday night. This discrepancy highlights a major flaw in Jewish and Zionist education, which hasn't provided a comprehensive framework to value multiple Zionist perspectives. My view is that Zionist education needs to redefine Zionism and reclaim it from both external and internal Jewish forces trying to distort its core principles.

Even acknowledging that such an analysis is reductive, contentious, and offensive to many, I propose five concrete actions that Jewish educators must take to preserve Zionism for at least another generation.

1. Reclaim the Israeli Flag

In education, symbols matter. In Israel, as in many other countries, no symbol is more prominent than the national flag. Over time, the Israeli flag has come to be displayed with pride in right-wing and Orthodox settings, both within Israel and across the Jewish world, but it should be prominently displayed in all Jewish educational environments. Similarly, just as the Israeli flag was reclaimed by the Israeli judicial reform protesters before October 7, all Jewish educational and communal settings must reclaim it as a symbol of Jewish freedom and self-determination.

2. Reclaim Zionist Education

Zionism was never a monolithic ideology. If Jewish educators do not teach the multiplicity of Zionist viewpoints, then under the current Israeli government our children will only be hearing the echoes of Jabotinsky,[160] Kook,[161] and Begin.[162] Our youth also need to be exposed to Borochov,[163] Gordon,[164] and Katznelson.[165] As much as I would like all Jewish youth to read Arthur Hertzberg's *The Zionist Idea* or Gil Troy's *The Zionist Ideas*,[166] I am realistic about the possibilities. But I am also determined to ensure that the values of all these classic thinkers permeate Jewish educator trainings and learning settings.

Exposing our youth to diverse Zionist viewpoints is crucial, but even more important is showing them how these visions of Israel can intersect, engage in respectful dialogue, and even critique one another. Jewish education offers a unique opportunity to excel in this area where the mainstream Jewish community often falls short. It must reject the dismissal of right-wing Jews as racist fascists and left-wing Jews as self-hating traitors. This education in various "Zionisms" teaches students how to debate and argue within a Jewish collective.

An Australian educator, Jeremy Stowe-Lindner, provides further context for how Zionism should be conceived and taught:

> But Zionism, like any political or ideological framework, does not exist in a vacuum. To teach Zionism responsibly in 2025 is to teach it as a love that is neither blind nor naïve. We teach it through the lens of the Holocaust, through Jewish migration stories, through poetry and politics, through Israeli music, and the lives of immigrants and sabras, and soldiers and citizens. And just as Australians teach about Australian history, British teach about British history, and Americans teach about American history, we teach it alongside its ethical burdens, its historical tensions, and its unresolved dreams.

> To love Israel is not to idolize it. Nor is it to immunize it from critique.[167]

3. Reclaim Israel's Declaration of Independence

There is no official document that declares Israel a Jewish democracy, but Israel's Declaration of Independence is as close as one gets:

> ERETZ-ISRAEL (The Land of Israel) was the birthplace of the Jewish people. Here their spiritual, religious, and political identity was shaped. Here they first attained to statehood, created cultural values of national and universal significance, and gave to the world the eternal Book of Books.
>
> This right is the natural right of the Jewish people to be masters of their own fate, like all other nations, in their own sovereign state.
>
> THE STATE OF ISRAEL will be open for Jewish immigration and for the Ingathering of the Exiles; it will foster the development of the country for the benefit of all its inhabitants; it will be based on freedom, justice, and peace as envisaged by the prophets of Israel; it will ensure complete equality of social and political rights to all its inhabitants irrespective of religion, race, or sex; it will guarantee freedom of religion, conscience, language, education, and culture; it will safeguard the Holy Places of all

> religions; and it will be faithful to the principles of the Charter of the United Nations.

As Jewish educators, Israel's Declaration of Independence should be an integral part of the core canon of Jewish literacy. It serves as a reminder that Israel is a relatively young nation, less than eighty-years-old, and that the Declaration of Independence is a document of vision. This understanding is crucial for educators who work with Jewish students today.

Dr. David Breakstone, former Deputy Chairman of the World Zionist Organization, wrote of Israel, "Our society must be characterized by moral, social, and humanitarian values. The vision of an exemplary society is not an aspiration to be relegated to some far-off utopian future, but a necessary condition for our survival."[168]

Our learners must understand that Israel, like every other nation, is not perfect, but it possesses an aspirational vision that is worth striving toward.

4. Reclaim Brandeisian Zionism

One of the most important Zionist thinkers to teach our learners today is the late U.S. Supreme Court Justice Louis Brandeis, who wrote: "Let no American imagine that Zionism is inconsistent with patriotism.... Every American Jew who aids in advancing the Jewish settlement in Palestine...will likewise be a better man and a better American."[169]

Jewish educators must clearly communicate to learners that Zionism and patriotism can coexist and thrive. While we must teach about such events as the Dreyfus Affair,[170] this is a sensitive issue today, as accusations of Jewish disloyalty to their country have resurfaced in the post-October 7 world.[171]

For Jewish educators, this discussion should focus on Israel's overall significance for Jews today. While some in Israel and the Jewish community believe Israel is the only place where Jews can live a full Jewish life, others see it as just another Jewish community. Educators must facilitate discussions that include all these perspectives and more. Brandeis's insights are crucial to making this a comprehensive conversation.

5. Reclaim Cultural Zionism

Other, less political Zionists who need to be embraced by Jewish educators are "cultural Zionists" like Ahad Ha'Am[172] and Eliezer Ben Yehuda.[173] Even if Israel is viewed merely as another Jewish community globally, the revival of Jewish culture and language in Israel stands as one of the most significant achievements of the Jewish people in the past century. Jewish educators should prioritize teaching Hebrew, with a strong focus on modern conversational Hebrew. Israeli culture, expressed through art, film, television, poetry, and music, should be integral to Jewish education. The influence of culture in education is immense, and its potential in Israel education is vast.[174] This is why it was important for me to feature iconic Israeli cartoonist Shoshke (Zeev Engelmeyer) on the front cover of this book. For many Israelis and Jews around the world, his cartoons fast became enduring markers this time - especially capturing the profound light, resilience, and humanity of the hostages during the intense and unforgettable events of the post October 7 world.

Such is the significance of culture in Israel education that, at one stage of my writing, the tentative title of this book was *Even Better*, a loose translation of the Hebrew phrase "*od yoter tov*," the refrain of Yair Elitzur's song "Tamid Ohev Oti" ("He always loves me"), which emerged as an unofficial anthem in Israel and around the Jewish world in the aftermath of October 7. More than simple optimism, the phrase captured a posture that feels both honest and aspirational: not naïve certainty that everything *will* be good, but a commitment to believing that something better is still possible.

Years ago, this book might have been called *Yihiye Tov* ("It will be good"), echoing the confident hope of Yehonatan Geffen and David Broza's famous song. But the world has changed. In a moment defined by rupture, grief, and moral complexity, *Even Better* reflects a quieter, more resilient hope; one that acknowledges pain while insisting that educators must continue to imagine and work toward something better than what is. Yet it was dismissed as the book title because ultimately "better still" is an inadequate translation that fails to capture the deeper emotional tenor and significance of the Hebrew "*od yoter tov.*"

* * *

When we think about recharging Zionist education, there are at least two "elephants in the room" that must be acknowledged.

First, the era of Zionism, as a twentieth-century movement, may have already reached its peak and could now be in rapid decline or in need of major transformation. Although this discussion might fall outside the typical focus of most Jewish educators, recognizing that Israel could simply be one Jewish community among many, albeit with unique characteristics, carries significant implications for Jewish education.

Second, there is a growing number of non-Zionist and anti-Zionist Jews today. It is crucial to acknowledge that this increase is particularly noticeable among younger Jews, who were often considered the most dedicated members of their generation. For example, there are reports of Jewish professionals "who describe being fired, quitting under pressure, or seeing their roles disappear since October 7 for issues surrounding criticism of Israel or support for a permanent ceasefire."[175]

As Jewish educators, we cannot ignore that many Jews live a full Jewish life without any connection to Israel. We must also acknowledge that some Jews do not want a Jewish state to exist at all.

In response to these challenges, I offer three principles for educators:

1. Articulate clearly who you are and where you stand on Israel. Ensure that all stakeholders in your organization share these views and will support you in upholding them.
2. Create Jewish education spaces that allow all participants to feel safe, heard, and respected.
3. Be prepared to enforce boundaries and perimeters.

A successful Israel and Zionist education program must clearly define both what it stands for and what it opposes or will not tolerate. Some organizations may find it helpful to distinguish between voices they are willing to accept and those they are willing to actively platform. Others may determine that simply maintaining civility is sufficient to ensure diversity. Whatever approach an organization chooses, it should establish these guidelines transparently, enabling educators to operate effectively within the defined framework.

* * *

When it comes to bridging the gap between Jews living abroad and Israelis, there's no other initiative that compares to the profound impact of the "Israel experience."

Jews have been visiting and touring Israel since long before the state was officially established. The term "Israel experience" became popular in the 1980s, referring to educational travel programs designed to help participants explore Israel and strengthen their identity, typically within the context of a peer group.

There are many examples of these programs, including Taglit Birthright Israel, MASA, RootOne, Honeymoon Israel, and Momentum. While these programs differ in their target populations, they reflect similar pedagogies that blend touring, educational programs, and social experiences. All strive to give the participants as authentic an Israel experience as possible. One of their key features is the *mifgash* (encounter), a structured, facilitated encounter between Israelis and Jews from abroad.

If no other educational program rivals the Israel experience, why shouldn't we focus our efforts on ensuring that every Israel educational initiative prioritizes sending people to Israel as its main goal? Just as we can't expect the same results from Jewish education in different settings—such as day school versus camp—we shouldn't expect lower-intensity Israel education initiatives to achieve outcomes comparable to those of a multi-week experience of learning, touring, and living in Israel.

This orientation would not only give Israel educators, including *shlichim*[176] and *shinshinim*,[177] a tangible outcome to pursue but create a pathway of experiences leading up to a pinnacle event for Jewish learners. Moreover, an individual's Israel experience doesn't have to be limited to one. A life journey from a teen program to experiencing Israel as a young adult and even older is a logical trajectory for someone on their continued Israel and Jewish educational journey.

Jewish peoplehood education and Zionist education must undergo a comprehensive philosophical and pedagogical change. These concepts embody the ideals and aspirations of Jewish identity in the contemporary world, and Jewish educators are uniquely equipped to present and articulate their transformation.

Questions to Consider

- When in your life have you felt the closest connection to and conversely the furthest distance from Jews around the world and from Israelis?
- What does Zionism mean to you and how have you reacted and responded when your understanding of Zionism has been questioned or challenged by others?

9

Recharging *Hasbara* in Israel Education

In the immediate aftermath of October 7, I received numerous requests from various segments of the Jewish community to establish more Israel education programs for young people.

However, in many cases, it quickly became clear that the requests were actually for training programs aimed at empowering young people to defend Israel when it faced criticism and vilification on college campuses and in schools.

However, *hasbara*, Israel advocacy, while critical in today's world, is not Israel education.

For a couple of years, I had a pretty good side gig. Schools, synagogues, and campus and adult education groups would pay me to teach them how to defend Israel. I had a flashy PowerPoint presentation with all the right talking points. My proposal was relatively simple: If someone says X to you, respond with Y.

If they say, "Israel has no right to exist," you respond, "Yes, it does, UN Security Council Resolution 242 (1967) and 338 (1973) endorses 'every State in the area and their right to live in peace within secure and recognized boundaries free from threats or acts of force.'"[178]

If they say, "Zionism is racism," you respond, "No, it isn't. Israeli Arabs are equal citizens of the State of Israel."

If they persist, you continue, "By the way, even Martin Luther King Jr. was a supporter of Zionism, so how could it be racist? He even said, 'Peace for Israel means security, and we must stand with all our might to protect its right to exist, its territorial integrity, and the right to use whatever sea lanes it needs. Israel is one of the great outposts of democracy in the world.'"[179]

I firmly believed that young Jews, armed with these talking points, would become stronger, more committed, and prouder Jews, as well as staunch supporters of Israel. This wasn't just about changing minds; I genuinely thought these talking points would empower them.

Unfortunately, I was wrong. Talking points seldom, if ever, change people's minds. People increasingly live within the echo chambers of their social media algorithms, which only reinforce their existing opinions, making contrary talking points largely irrelevant. Moreover, it is particularly alarming to realize that providing people, especially today's younger generation, with talking points often does not bring them closer to Israel. In fact, it might have the opposite effect, causing them to turn away from Israel entirely due to their inherent disdain for authority figures dictating what they should know, think, and do.

Many Israel educators, including myself, recognized the flaws in the advocacy-based approach to Israel long before October 7. However, in recent months, there has been a renewed promotion of advocacy programs aimed specifically at Jewish youth and young adults. I hope this chapter serves as a warning to the Jewish community that necessary Israel advocacy should not be confused with essential Israel education.

***

Hasbara is related to the verb *le'hasbir*, "to explain." The word is most commonly used to describe Israel's public diplomacy efforts—both by the government and by private individuals—to explain or justify Israel's policies and actions to international audiences. Sometimes called "public relations" or, more cynically, "propaganda," the underlying assumption of *hasbara* has always been that, if one could just explain something clearly to Israel's opponents, they would change their minds.

We can quibble about the term itself but, fundamentally, I believe that advocating for Israel is a good thing. It is important for Israel's side to be explained to multiple audiences. People should be trained and equipped to lobby politicians, speak to media outlets, and generally be prepared to explain Israel's policies and actions. Importantly, explaining is not the same as defending, justifying, or apologizing.

But hasbara is not education. At best, *hasbara* might be one of the options learners consider pursuing after receiving a comprehensive Israel education. Many educators have said similar things, including Dr. Noam Weissman, whose own organization, OpenDor Media has undergone several changes in relation to the distinction between advocacy and education. Even though much of OpenDor's work equips people to be better Israel advocates, Weissman staunchly believes that, "Israel education is not about advocacy. It's about cultivating a relationship with Israel that is authentic, nuanced, and grounded in Jewish identity."[180]

Importantly, no one's initial encounter with Israel is through being trained as an advocate, except, as I jokingly say, for those who are direct descendants of AIPAC.[181] Furthermore, organizations that impose advocacy approaches on today's youth and young adults risk alienating them entirely. This generation is often described as distrustful of institutions and constantly seeking values-driven responses rather than facts delivered by authority figures.[182]

There are also some fundamental changes taking place in the world that greatly impact the role of *hasbara*.

When I was growing up in Australia, I learned very quickly about two foundational rules that guided the discourse on Israel in the Jewish sphere.

The first rule was that Jews living outside of Israel should consistently support the democratically elected Israeli government of the time.

The second rule was that, while individuals might disagree with specific Israeli policies, they should refrain from engaging in public debates about them, as this could be perceived as washing Israel's dirty laundry in public.

Many people today still adhere to these principles, often out of fear that Israel's adversaries will interpret such public criticism as a sign of weakness and exploit it against Israel and the Jewish community. However, as educational principles, these rules are misguided and no longer relevant to most young Jews today. As Tal Becker, vice-president of the Shalom Hartman Institute, said, "Even the belief that we shouldn't air our dirty laundry in public shouldn't be an excuse not to do the laundry."[183]

It is important to acknowledge that the "rules" mentioned above were created in the twentieth century, when journalism, news, expertise, and facts had very different meanings than they do today. Although we might nostalgically recall the "good ol' days," we risk overlooking the new rules (or lack thereof) that make social media, influencers, and artificial intelligence far more influential on our learners' lives than any educational intervention we could possibly imagine.

We might have once decided to try to maintain forward-facing unity, and only discuss certain issues in public. But that era is over for a generation that is more likely to learn about events in Israel from their cellphones and not in a classroom or at a family meal.

As educators, our utmost responsibility is to equip our learners with the skills to discern between positive and negative content on social media platforms. It is not enough to simply label Dua Lipa, who currently boasts approximately 87.6 million followers on Instagram, as wrong and antisemitic when she posts, "Burning children alive can never be justified. The whole world is mobilizing to stop the Israeli genocide. Please show your solidarity with Gaza."[184]

Moreover, since Israel has been led by right-wing governments for much of the past three decades, there is a risk that discussions about *hasbara* could become partisan.

It can be argued that more conservative Jews support *hasbara* because they generally agree with many of the sentiments and actions of the Israeli government over the past thirty years. Conversely, progressives might recoil from *hasbara* because it places them in the uncomfortable and often intolerable position of defending a government whose core values they often oppose.

For these reasons, many Israel educators avoid engaging in *hasbara*-style activities, arguing that they have become so closely associated with a right-wing agenda that they cannot be adapted into an inclusive approach for Israel education.

Instead of advocating a complete separation between *hasbara* and Israel education, as educators have tried to do over the past few years, I propose a different approach. I believe there can be a new understanding of *hasbara* that will withstand partisanship, regardless of the Israeli government of the day.

* * *

It is incumbent upon Jewish educators to offer *hasbara* as one viable pathway for learners to actively express their commitment to Israel and the Jewish people, so long as we redefine what it means to advocate for Israel.

This new approach to Israel education should be comprehensive enough to go beyond just reacting to misinformation about Israel. While I am undecided about whether to continue using the term "*hasbara*," the essential aspect of this new approach is to move away from *hasbara* that serves the Israeli government's interests. Instead, it should enable individuals to support and represent the entire Israeli people.

Jewish educators should never have sought to create a cadre of Jews capable of defending and lobbying for the actions of the Israeli government. If learners choose to advocate for the Israeli leadership due to a good education, and they genuinely believe that certain decisions, policies, and actions of the Israeli government warrant defense, that is a positive outcome.

Similarly, if a Jew outside of Israel feels compelled to explain, defend, and advocate for the beliefs and viewpoints of the Israeli opposition or a minority perspective held by segments of the Israeli population, that should be equally celebrated.

I understand the concerns of the Jewish community regarding the potential consequences of publicly criticizing the current Israeli government's policies and actions. However, I firmly believe that education should not present only one ideological or political viewpoint as the sole positive outcome. In fact, such an approach can be detrimental and even dangerous.

I understand that some may find this concept challenging. I have frequently been asked, "Why should we train Jews to speak out against the Israeli government when CNN, the BBC, and the New York Times are doing the job for us?" However, I am writing as a Jewish educator, not as a lobbyist or spokesperson for the current Israeli government.

Good education empowers learners to explore diverse viewpoints, enabling them to reach their own informed conclusions. Bad education imposes a singular perspective on a complex situation, discouraging any deviation by threatening ostracization. This is not education; it is indoctrination.

So let me offer a new definition: *Israel advocacy is the effort to promote the interests of Israelis, often by influencing public opinion, political policy, or educational narratives.*

Good Israel education should include developing learners' knowledge and skills to enable them to:

- Present the perspectives of Israelis in public discourse.
- Counter criticism of or misinformation about Israelis.
- Mobilize political, educational, or communal support for Israelis.
- Defend Israel's right to exist and defend itself as a Jewish and democratic state.
- Advocate for policies that align with the interests of Israelis.

In other words, Israel education should enable learners to represent all Israelis and not just the Israeli government.

To do this, Israel educators must convey to their learners that Israel is a highly diverse society made up of multiple overlapping demographic, religious, and cultural communities.

Roughly three-quarters of the Israeli population is Jewish (73–75 percent). Around 17–18 percent is Muslim, including the Bedouin community. About 2 percent is Christian and 1.5–2 percent is Druze.

Within the Jewish population, there is wide variation in religious identity and practice. Approximately 10–14 percent is ultra-Orthodox (Haredi). Some 10–12 percent is religious Zionist. Around 25–30 percent identify as "traditional" to varying degrees. Roughly 40–50 percent identify as secular.

In terms of ancestry, Israel includes large populations of Jews with Mizrahi and Sephardi roots (approximately 40–45 percent) and Ashkenazi origins (about 30–35 percent), as well as a visible Ethiopian community and a very significant population of Jews from the former Soviet Union.

Israel is also a markedly young society. Nearly 28 percent of the population is under the age of fifteen, around 60 percent is of working age, and about 12 percent is sixty-five or older.

Politically, Israeli society is deeply divided along lines of religion, ethnicity, and ideology. Secular, Haredi, Mizrahi, Ashkenazi, and immigrant communities often exhibit different patterns of party affiliation, policy priorities, and levels of support for the government.

Taken together, these layers of religion, ethnicity, culture, immigration history, and age create a complex and dynamic society that continues to shape Israel's internal debates, cultural creativity, and evolving relationship with Jews around the world.

All Israel education and *hasbara* must maintain a commitment to upholding Israel as a Jewish and democratic state. As we are reminded in Israel's Declaration of Independence, the Jewish state "will be based on freedom, justice and peace as envisaged by the prophets of Israel."[185] For those seeking more clarity, perhaps a framework that suggests that *hasbara* encompasses the viewpoints endorsed by all Zionist factions in the Knesset (the Israeli parliament) would be helpful.

We have reached a time when expecting uniformity among Jews living outside Israel is both unfair and unrealistic. This is crucial for effective Israel education, which should value and embrace the diversity of mindsets and opinions within Israel. By doing so, it can become mature enough to accept that such diversity also exists among Jews abroad. Those who prioritize Jewish unity, especially during wartime, must recognize that unity no longer requires uniformity.

Jewish learners who develop the ability to understand and advocate for the full complexity of Israeli society—its diverse identities, religions, cultures, political perspectives, and lived experiences—are uniquely equipped to build deeper, more authentic connections between Jews around the world and those in Israel.

Rather than seeing Israel as an abstract symbol or a one-dimensional political issue, these learners engage with it as a vibrant and multifaceted society composed of real people facing real challenges, tensions, and aspirations. This nuanced perspective fosters empathy, humility, and a sense of shared responsibility, helping Jews around the world move past defensiveness or idealization toward genuine, meaningful partnership.

At the same time, Israelis are more inclined to trust and feel seen by Jews around the world who genuinely possess knowledge of and care for the diverse aspects of Israeli life. This approach, grounded in complexity, honesty, and a sense of shared humanity, transforms the relationship from one of distant affiliation to a living, reciprocal connection.

It is difficult to underestimate the potential impact of this shift in the context of nearly three decades of right-leaning Israeli governments, even though education about Israel should ideally be approached in a non-partisan manner. For Jews who already feel a strong connection to the ideological right and to Israel's religious elements, little will change. What will change is that more diverse groups of Jews will now be able to cultivate similar relationships and commitments to other segments of Israeli society.

Some might argue that Jews should still simply support the democratically elected Israeli government of the day. In my experience, however, this stance is typically held only by those whose views align with the current leadership. For progressive Jews living outside Israel, the consequences of this new approach would be profound as it would amplify their voices in the effort to ensure that Israel remains a democracy that embraces the full diversity of its population.

In times of war, it is understandable why many in the Jewish community would strongly urge all Jews living outside Israel to unequivocally support the Israeli government and military. This is not a new phenomenon. It took place, for example, during and after the 1982 Lebanon War, when Jews around the world often expressed concern about and even protested the Israeli leadership, just like their Israeli counterparts.

However, the rules of Israel education should not solely revolve around adversity and threat. To be resilient, it must endure challenging times, but it should also be proactive, uniting Jews during both war and peace. Unfortunately, those demanding uniform support for Israel implicitly suppress dissent, which neither democracy nor effective education can tolerate.

This definition and understanding of *hasbara*, which involves advocating for a diverse range of Israelis, not just the Israeli government, represents a significant departure from traditional Jewish communal norms. However, it is important to recognize that this diversity of advocacy has been developing for decades. Now, particularly for Israel educators, it is crucial to embrace and promote this change. Over time, it will have a profound impact on the relationship between Jews around the world and Israelis.

While Israel educators cannot solve Israel's problems, they must ensure that all learners are able to find their voice when confronting these problems. Israel education, although rooted in the present, has the capacity to alter the relationship between Israelis and Jews outside of Israel for generations. Recharging *hasbara* can do just that.

Good Israel education must incorporate this new form of *hasbara* as one of its goals. If Jewish educators and the community fail to adapt to this new paradigm, they risk further alienating a significant percentage of the Jewish people.

Questions to Consider

- How important is Jewish unity to you?
- When it comes to issues facing Israel and the Jewish people, are there specific issues on which you feel obligated to take a stand, even when it dissents from those of your peers, colleagues, or communal and governmental leaders?

10

Recharging Listening and Empathy

I met Fred on the West Coast in the summer of 2025. He goes by "Fred" even though his name is Fareed, and he defines himself as a Palestinian from Dearborn, Michigan. An outgoing fifty-something man, it didn't take too long for Fareed to talk about his upcoming plans to take his aging mother to Jerusalem, where neither he nor she had been in over 40 years. They were supposed to go last year, but "you know, because of the situation," they delayed their trip.

I didn't really know how to respond to Fareed, but something told me that mentioning that I was a Zionist who had lived in Jerusalem for two years and had been there dozens of times since would not be productive.

Fareed was by no means the first Palestinian I ever met and interacted with, but this conversation stayed with me and still makes me uncomfortable. I never wanted my Zionism to be at the expense of someone else's attachment to the same land, but invariably it is and always will be.

Over the past two years, other encounters with Palestinians, Israeli Arabs,[186] Druze, and Bedouin have allowed me to consider "the other" and also reflect on aspects of my own identity.

In the immediate months after October 7, I found myself in Rahat. The largest Bedouin city in Israel, it lies approximately twenty kilometers from Beersheba and thirty kilometers from Gaza. In Arabic, *rahat* means "rest" or "comfort." It's true that some of the visit was filled with that. But most of it was deeply uncomfortable, which has troubled me ever since.

The story of the extended family I met with was written up in the *New York Times*:

> In daring acts, some Bedouin saved the lives of Jewish Israelis on Oct. 7.
>
> When Ismail Qrinawi, 45, and three other residents of Rahat heard the incessant rocket fire raining down on Israel that morning, they decided to travel to Kibbutz Beeri to rescue his cousin, who was working in the community's food hall.
>
> On the way, the four encountered terrified people fleeing the grounds of a music festival that had been invaded by militants, Mr. Qrinawi recalled. Without hesitation, they risked their lives to ferry dozens of them to safety in a Toyota Land Cruiser.
>
> "We saved their lives because they're people," Mr. Qrinawi said in an interview. "My responsibility as a person is to save anyone I can. It doesn't matter if you're a Jew or an Arab."[187]

When the five cousins, including the one rescued, met with us—a group of Jewish educators from North America—the room was filled with awe, respect, and admiration, not to mention quite a few tears. The discomfort came when one of the cousins explained why he risked his life to save people from the Nova music festival: "because of *Goral Yisrael*," the destiny of Israel.

This wasn't my first encounter with Bedouins. I've visited Israel numerous times and spent several nights sleeping in Bedouin tents at Kfar HaNokdim, near the base of Masada. However, this comment might be a bit facetious, considering that the tourist-oriented nature of the Bedouin tent experience is widely recognized within the Israel experience community.[188]

I was always aware of the issues faced by the Israeli Bedouin. Several years ago, I was particularly moved by a chapter about the Bedouin in Donna Rosenthal's excellent book *The Israelis*.[189] I've also been following recent news about the Bedouin population in Israel with great interest, particularly in relation to the interconnected issues of land ownership and polygamy,[190] as well the Nation-State Law.[191]

For a long time, I had an intellectual understanding that approximately 20 percent of Israel's population is Arab, with around 4 percent being Bedouin. However, in my mind, the Bedouins were always considered "the other," rarely part of the Israeli population that the average tourist has authentic encounters with. Hearing the words "*Goral Yisrael*" spoken in Hebrew by an Israeli Bedouin, and realizing that this very Jewish phrase unites us as part of our collective destiny, was a transformative experience for me. As our children would say, I was "mind blown."

The twenty-first century has been characterized as an era where most of us reside in our comfortable bubbles and echo chambers. This often results in encounters with "the other," whoever that may be, becoming opportunities for not only learning about someone else but also for profound self-reflection.[192]

I recognize that this chapter is of an increasingly countercultural nature. However, it is a mandate I propose for all education, particularly Jewish and Israeli education. As challenging as it may be, especially in the aftermath of October 7, listening to the "other" and, perhaps, even at times empathizing with them must become a crucial aspect of all effective Israel education.

* * *

Listening to "the other" has always been closely linked to what I view as effective education. Martin Buber's philosophy of dialogue provides a strong basis for understanding why this is a crucial aspect of meaningful education. In his influential work *I and Thou*, Buber differentiates between "I–It" relationships, where we treat others as objects to be analyzed or used, and "I–Thou" relationships, where we engage with the other as a complete, irreducible person.

Education grounded in an "I–Thou" approach necessitates profound, open listening; not merely to respond or correct, but to genuinely engage with the other person's lived experience, perspective, and humanity. As Buber wrote, "all real living is meeting."[193] This implies that genuine learning occurs through authentic relationships rather than just the transfer of information. When educators adopt a dialogical approach, they establish environments where differences are seen as opportunities for growth, empathy, and transformation. This allows learners to view each other not as adversaries or problems to resolve, but as partners in a collective human search for meaning.

Listening can and should take place in all human interactions, including serendipitous ones. I was reminded of this when my former colleague Suri Jacknis once asked me how much I knew about the person from whom I had purchased my breakfast every day for the past three years. I was shocked when I realized I didn't even know Providencia's name—and she was wearing a name tag.

Nel Noddings, a leading educational philosopher, asserts that listening plays a critical role in the ethic of care that is central to effective education. Listening embodies relational ethics by allowing teachers to truly understand students as individuals with unique experiences and needs. Noddings argues that the role of the educator is not only to impart knowledge but also to cultivate trust, empathy, and ethical growth, making it an essential practice in classrooms committed to care.[194]

A commitment to care is vital when incorporating diverse voices in educational environments. These voices should not merely serve as props to enliven the classroom; they must be treated with the same respect and compassion we expect from others.

However, while listening might be one necessary step for educators, sometimes there might be a need to take the process to the next level. In 2015, The Jewish Education Project presented a Jewish Futures Conference entitled "Radical Empathy," with the issue of Israel consciously not on the agenda.

It was a period in America when race-based police shootings dominated the news, and the most "radical" speaker at our event was a policewoman who had shot a black teenager while on duty. Although she was cleared of any wrongdoing, hearing her perspective was a novel experience for most of our audience. Listening to someone whose voice is rarely heard was eye-opening, helping me gain a deeper understanding of the daily challenges faced by police officers. It also transformed me, revealing my blind spots and showing how much of my perspective had been shaped by the bubbles and algorithms in which I live.

Listening to others is crucial for effective education, but empathy may not always be necessary or beneficial. Hearing someone's story doesn't mean you have to adopt their pain or suffering, although some compassionate learners may reach that conclusion after hearing the narrative. This chapter will examine four areas where I believe listening is essential, and where empathy might also be important, or even critical, for successful Israel education: the divides between learners and Palestinians, religious groups, generations, and Zionists.

The Palestinian Narrative

Regarding the Palestinian narrative, I have been greatly influenced by my good friend and colleague Yona Shem-Tov, the CEO of Encounter. Encounter's mission is to develop informed, courageous, and resilient Jewish communal leadership by engaging with the full complexity of the Israeli-Palestinian reality. Yona's research interests have consistently centered on empathically engaging with others as an end in itself and as a way to better understand oneself.

My journey with Encounter to east Jerusalem, Ramallah, and Bethlehem gave me the opportunity to listen to Palestinians in their homes and on their land. As an Israel educator, I can spend hours drawing maps for my students and discussing whether these areas should be referred to as the West Bank, Judaea and Samaria, Yehuda v'Shomron, or the occupied territories. Now these maps are filled with real voices.

One specific example draws attention to how experiential education resonates in different ways for different learners. In February 2025, Mahmoud Muna's bookstore in eastern Jerusalem was raided, and he and his nephew were arrested by Israeli police, who claimed that the materials sold could incite violence. The raid sparked international condemnation, with critics claiming that it represented a broader assault on freedom of expression and Palestinian cultural life,[195] Yet Mahmoud is someone many Jews outside of Israel, including myself, have met on several occasions, such is his willingness to share his story with all who are prepared to listen. So, the raid on his bookstore resonated very differently for those who had a personal connection with Mahmoud.

Listening to and empathizing with "the other" can be essential tools in Israel education. However, Israel educators should not only focus on the Palestinian narrative. There are many other voices in our lives that we often choose to ignore, either implicitly or explicitly. Although Jewish education is not meant to solve all the world's problems, I suggest that teaching our learners to listen to others will provide them with invaluable life skills and contribute to making communities and the world better.

It is understandable that the months after October 7 have not necessarily been the right time to advocate for the inclusion of more Palestinian narratives in Jewish education. For others, however, it seems like the perfect time. The reality is that calls for Jewish youth to learn more about the Palestinian narrative predate October 7. This is yet another reason why Israel education must strive to become proactive rather than reactive.

Just as there is no single Israeli or Jewish story, there is no single Palestinian voice. This is important to understand and accept, though it's hard for those who believe all Palestinians support Hamas and want to destroy the Jewish state. It also speaks to the limits of empathy. I might be willing to listen and try to understand someone else's point of view, so long as they don't want me dead.

I don't intend to draw any moral or political equivalence, but I must be honest and acknowledge that there are also violent

Jewish extremists, possibly those known as the "hilltop youth,"[196] whom I would find difficult to meet with in search of empathy. In my view, the morality of education is crucial for effective learning. One of my firm boundaries is the explicit promotion of violence motivated by race, religion, or ethnicity, which I consider unacceptable and will not endorse in an educational environment.

These internal discussions brought back memories of my time as a Holocaust Studies student and teacher. The question that frequently arose was whether we could ever attempt to comprehend the mindset of the Nazis. On my podcast "Adapting: The Future of Jewish Education," my guest Rabbi Dr. Laura Novak Winer argued—largely but not solely from a theological perspective—that "All people have an element of goodness inside of them," even Hamas terrorists.[197] I cannot accept such a sentiment, and I find it unacceptable to expect that any Jewish educator would even try to comprehend what I view as the pure inhuman evil of Hamas.

Despite these limitations, I do recognize that advocating for Jewish youth to understand the Palestinian narrative is a political statement. This aligns with my belief that all education is political, as educators constantly make decisions about what to impart to future generations, which reflect the society they envision for the future.[198]

Incorporating the Palestinian narrative into Jewish and Israel education at least recognizes that there are two groups vying for the same land. This is arguably one of the most weighted political statements possible today. Thus, it cannot and should not be avoided in the context of good Israel education.

Certain voices gain prominence due to their significant influence and sway over specific segments of the population. While even acknowledging Rashid Khalidi, a distinguished

Palestinian-American historian and professor at Columbia University, may be triggering for some, we must acknowledge his powerful and influential voice in Palestinian discourse:

> The Palestinians were not passive victims of a historical process over which they had no control. They were active agents in their own history, struggling to preserve their land, their homes, their livelihoods, and their dignity. The Zionist project was not merely a national movement but a colonial enterprise that sought to displace the indigenous population and establish a Jewish state in their place. The Palestinians resisted this project from the very beginning, and their resistance continues to this day.[199]

I acknowledge that statements like these can be jarring for some Jewish readers. I also recognize that some readers may immediately reject the idea of teaching this perspective. If you firmly believe that all Palestinians seek Israel's complete destruction and that all Arabs wish for the worldwide annihilation of Jews, I disagree with you, but I will always strive to empathize with you. This is partly because, especially after October 7, I have experienced similar fleeting thoughts. However, if you are a Jewish educator, even if you personally hold these beliefs, I urge you to continue reading for the benefit of your students. Understanding these different perspectives is critical and our learners deserve to hear it first in the safe and nurturing environments we strive to create.

For many years, much of Israel education has been filled with myths. Take, for example, two famous quotes often cited in many Israel education curricula:

"A land without a people for a people
without a land."[200] —early Zionist slogan
"The Arabs never miss an opportunity to miss
an opportunity."[201] —Abba Eban, 1973

When education is reduced to quotes and slogans, it becomes a collection of generalizations and the teaching of mythology instead of history. In both cases, the underlying ideological influences are evident, reflecting mainstream Israel and Zionist education over many decades, especially since 1967. This approach has largely attempted to overlook and discredit the Palestinian people in its curriculum. It is important to note that while both quotes are valuable for teaching, they also deserve to be discussed and debated.

Such is the challenge for Israel educators, who are often navigating a delicate balance between teaching myth and reality. This tension is essential, as it is with most national stories that rely on at least some form of mythology as part of their origin story.

Joseph Campbell, an American scholar of comparative mythology and religion, once said, "Myths are not lies, but imaginative narratives that societies create to explain their origins, values, and place in the cosmos; they provide a framework through which communities understand themselves and their history."[202] It is essential for educators to understand this.

Teaching the mythology of Zionism and Israel can be challenging for Jewish educators. This is partly because it is often assumed that this mythology devalues Palestinian national claims. At other times, the mythology does not reflect today's reality.

Dr. Alick Isaacs, a lecturer at the Hebrew University of Jerusalem's Melton Center for Jewish Education, wrote in a journal dedicated to Israel and Zionist education in Jewish day schools,

> The question of Israel education is difficult, not because educators need to choose between teaching the myth and the reality, but because the confusion caused by the coexistence of an ideology with its realization is blinding.... The challenge of Israel education...is the challenge of unraveling the confusion between ideology and reality in order to begin the search for a new ideological purpose that Israel's future can "stand for" in American Jewish life.[203]

In a post-October 7 world, it is crucial to engage with the Palestinian narrative. As Jewish youth enter college and increasingly high school, they will encounter terms like *nakba*, *Deir Yassin*, *Sabra and Shatilla*, and now *Rafah*. These terms are often presented in antagonistic or hostile ways, so it is preferable for our youth to learn about them first in the safe and brave environments of Jewish education.

I also suggest that Israel education should consider the voices of others, not just the Palestinian or Arab. We all have many "others" in our world. A successful Israel education should develop a will and pedagogy to uncover the many voices that define the diversity that is Israel. It must also recognize that what is "other" to some will be familiar to others, and vice-versa. This will help us learn about those who are close to us or our people and better understand ourselves. Two such divides worth considering are religious and generational.

The Religious Divide

Examining the religious divides within the Jewish people is integral to Israel education. These divides manifest on the question of "religion and state," in which Israel's Jewish nature impacts personal and societal issues. Understanding these issues is crucial for comprehending how Israeli society is constituted.

For Jews around the world, these debates often become contentious, as many come from non-Orthodox communities or countries where church and state are separated. To grapple with this, educators can bring in authentic voices to represent distinct arguments on the issue. At other times, activities can be designed to allow participants to view the issue from various perspectives.

These perspectives allow for a greater exploration of some of the key laws and documents that define the Jewish state, including the Law of Return,[204] the Status Quo Agreement,[205] and the Nation State Law.[206] They also allow for discussions of more contentious issues, including the recent push to conscript Haredim into the IDF.

Educators often use specific real-life scenarios to help learners develop empathy for multiple perspectives on these complex issues.

Scenario #1: The Red Sea Hotel Debate

It's December 31 at the Red Sea Hotel in Eilat, a popular tourist destination. The hotel is certified kosher by Israel's Chief Rabbinate, which means it must comply with religious standards for food and certain holiday observances. The Chief Rabbinate is threatening to revoke the hotel's kosher license because the hotel is celebrating the secular new year, which some believe has historical origins in Christian Europe. The Rabbinate argues that such practices should not be considered kosher in the Jewish state. In response, the hotel asserts that in a democratic state, all individuals and establishments should have the freedom to celebrate whatever and however they wish.

Scenario #2: Tisha B'Av in Tel Aviv[207]

Tel Aviv city inspectors issue 750 shekel fines to numerous restaurants and bars that remain open on the eve of Tisha B'Av. Traditionally, this marks the beginning of a fast day on which it is illegal for Jewish cities and towns to serve food and drink under Israeli law. This situation mirrors the Red Sea hotel New Year's Eve incident, highlighting the conflict between Orthodox religious authorities and the country's democratic values.

In 2025, two years after October 7, tensions escalate. Tisha B'Av occurs one day after Hamas releases heartbreaking videos of starved hostages Evyatar David and Rom Braslavski. Amidst this, a secular Tel Aviv city council member asks an Orthodox councilman, "But isn't it also the law for people like you to enlist in the army?"

The relationship between religion and state has always been contentious in Israeli society. However, against the backdrop of the ongoing war against Hamas and the divisions over

> whether Haredim should serve in the Israeli army, the stakes in these discussions become even more volatile and often more personal.

Allowing learners to view scenarios like this from multiple perspectives enhances their understanding of the larger issues at work and fosters empathy and respect for the stakeholders involved. Educationally, this process can be profound, it especially challenges pre-existing values and beliefs. For many Jews these issues are central as to why they feel so connected to Israel, and for others these very same issues are what makes them feel distanced, alienated and ostracized from the Jewish State.

The Generational Divide

As a proponent of innovation, I have been known to be dismissive of the "old ways." Indeed, I am averse to people who say of things that must change, "That's how they've always been done." Nevertheless, I try to remind myself, with a bit more humility, that perhaps King Solomon was right when he wrote, "What has been will be again, what has been done will be done again; there is nothing new under the sun."[208]

Ongoing surveys and research are continuing to show distinct generational divides on issues related to Israel and Palestine[209]. Engaging constructively with different perspectives, sometimes represented by generational divides, is a natural part of respectful disagreement. However, dismissing people's lived experience and its context is not acceptable.

This issue became clearer to me during recent discussions and debates about Israel's and America's recent attacks on Iran's nuclear program. The term "existential threat" was frequently used by politicians, news outlets, and ordinary people. I kept trying to understand the term as something that should be based on data. How much uranium did Iran actually possess? How close were they to developing nuclear weapons? I attempted to clarify semantic differences between terms like "imminent," "pre-emptive," and "proactive."

However, in a conversation with an older individual, the child of Holocaust survivors and a veteran of the Israeli wars of 1967 and 1973, I understood that our discussion was not merely about statistics and terminology. For him, it was deeply emotional, even visceral. No amount of so-called objective data could convince him of anything other than the existential threat Iran posed to Israel's survival. This experience was yet another reminder that the society we inhabit often dismisses the lived experience of older generations.

The Zionist Divide

Throughout this book, I have mentioned non-Zionists and anti-Zionists. I have suggested that Israel education should be guided by Zionist principles, although the term itself needs recharging.

I have indicated that those who identify as non-Zionists might be more integral to the Israeli narrative than they realize. However, telling someone they have misclassified themselves is not an effective educational approach. While I personally find anti-Zionists problematic, I believe their voices should be heard within educational frameworks.

Effective education cannot dismiss or silence dissenting opinions. At the same time, it is important to recognize that, in good education, not everyone must agree, argument can be essential, and not all voices require equal attention.

In my calls to include dissenting voices within the Jewish and Israel education frameworks, however, I may be surrendering to a noisy minority. I may have overcompensated to a point of neglecting the Zionist, an essential voice for whom many Jewish educators have become "the other."

After October 7, Yoni Heilman, an American-born Israeli soldier, began sending nearly daily WhatsApp updates to his family and friends in order to "clear [his] mind enough to sleep for a few hours."[210] His threads were soon read by thousands and Yoni became a way for many Jews living outside of Israel to feel what life was really like on the front lines.

Yoni wrote, "I am here, immersed in the exhausting, stressful, but fulfilling job of restoring security and peace for the Jewish people. Playing a small but defined role fulfilling: 'The hope of 2,000 years, to be a free people in our land,'" a line from "Hatikvah," Israel's national anthem.[211]

In today's social media-driven world, it has become increasingly easy for Jews living outside Israel to impose their values and ideologies on Israel and the Middle East. While it is important for these individuals to have and express their opinions, it is equally crucial for Israel education to embrace all voices, including Zionist ones, in every educational experience related to Israel. This is one reason why *shlichim*, or Israeli emissaries, play a vital role in the Jewish educational system worldwide, and why all experiences in Israel should involve genuine interactions with Israelis.

A note of caution for Israel educators: They should be aware that listening to a single Israeli voice does not provide a comprehensive understanding of Israeli society. Israel is home to numerous voices, including many dissenting ones, which often do not listen to each other. This chapter emphasizes the importance of listening and empathy in Israel education but listening and empathy are very relevant to broader societal contexts in Israel and Jewish communities worldwide.

* * *

Toward Listening and Radical Empathy

In the aftermath of Yitzhak Rabin's assassination in 1995, the following passages were taught by many Jewish educators around the world:

> Why has the first Temple fallen? Because there were three things: idolatry, adultery, and bloodshed.... But the second Temple, where the occupations were study of the Law, religious duties, and charity—why fell it? Because there was groundless enmity. From this we can infer that unfounded hatred is equal to all the three sins together: idolatry, adultery, and bloodshed.
> — Babylonian Talmud, Yoma, 9B[212]

> The Second Temple was destroyed because of senseless hatred. Perhaps the Third will be rebuilt because of causeless love.
> — Rav Abraham Isaac Kook, first Ashkenazi chief rabbi of British Mandatory Palestine

Whether it's our argumentative nature (two Jews, three opinions) or the capacity for anyone to hold a bullhorn in this age of social media, it has been a particularly bad few years for Jewish communal discourse. At times, the vitriol and venom, especially but not restricted to issues surrounding Israel, have been so bad that I've wondered whether this would be the moment of the Temple's destruction had it not already happened.

During a recent Passover seder, my family followed our tradition of identifying a contemporary plague affecting our world. I proposed "confirmation bias." This is the tendency for people to seek out and surround themselves with others who share similar opinions, reinforcing their existing views on various topics. The increasing number of opportunities to do this make us more resistant to change. This modern-day plague seems more potent than ever.

What if empathy became the central value of our time? What might change if we truly saw the world through perspectives other than our own? Imagine if we recognized that stepping into someone else's shoes and understanding their point of view was not just valuable, but essential to creating stronger communities and a better world. Genuine listening, in the spirit of Martin Buber's concept of the "I-Thou" encounter, is the first step in education. Yet it is the wholehearted embrace of empathy that holds the potential to transform education, deepen individual relationships, and even reshape communities, society, and the world.

I am not so unrealistic as to believe that we will ever collectively attain pervasive unconditional empathy or love for one another. However, I am hopeful enough to acknowledge the transformative power of empathy in our community, which is an essential step forward if we wish to return to an era of civility and thoughtful exchange of ideas.

Jewish learning becomes most meaningful when we begin by meeting learners where they truly are and using that as the foundation for their educational experiences. Teaching empathy is especially valuable because, when it develops into a life skill, it equips learners of all ages to view the world through multiple perspectives.

Listening is a skill that can be learned and developed. So is empathy, even if it is uncomfortable, difficult, and challenging.

Israel education stands at a crossroads and is in urgent need of recharging. To move forward, we must prioritize listening and embracing empathy. By challenging ourselves to see issues from multiple perspectives, we can not only enhance the quality of learning but also grow as individuals and foster more vibrant and dynamic communities.

Questions to Consider

- When has listening to someone else altered the way you think and feel about a particular issue?
- What are your own limits?
- When would you listen to someone else but never allow yourself to empathize with their views?

11

Recharging Jewish Joy and Pride

עִבְדוּ אֶת־יְהוָה בְּשִׂמְחָה

"Ivdu et Hashem b'simcha, bo'u lefanav birnana"
"Serve the LORD with gladness; come
before His presence with singing."
Psalms 100:2[213]

Eden Golan's performance at the Eurovision Song Contest 2024 in Malmö, Sweden was a moment of profound pride and unity for Jews and Israelis worldwide.

Representing Israel with her song "Hurricane," Golan captivated audiences not only with her vocal talent but also her resilience in the face of adversity. Despite facing significant challenges, including political protests and public criticism, Golan stood firm, delivering a performance that resonated deeply with her supporters.

Her graceful handling of the situation and her dedication to her craft earned her widespread admiration. In Israel, her performance was met with overwhelming support. Many saw her as a symbol of strength and perseverance. Israeli Prime Minister Benjamin Netanyahu praised Golan, stating, "They booed you and we shouted 'douze points' [12 points].... You have brought immense pride to the State of Israel."

Golan's participation in Eurovision 2024 not only showcased her musical talents but also highlighted the power of art to inspire joy, even in the face of adversity.

The concept of joy as a spiritual imperative in Jewish life is most vividly expressed by the Hasidic movement, which emerged in the late eighteenth and early nineteenth centuries. Rabbi Yisroel Baal Shem Tov (1698–1760), the movement's founder, taught that serving God with joy (*b'simchah*) was a divine commandment. In *Hasidut*, joy is often expressed through prayer, song, and dance.

Though some, especially Jewish youth, might see this as a call for more singing and dancing, this theology of joy is a counterbalance to the doom and gloom in which the Jewish community is often mired.

This does not minimize the significant rise in antisemitism in the United States and around the world. While completely stopping antisemitism may be beyond our capacities, we have substantial influence over how our community chooses to respond. In particular, Jewish educators play a key role in shaping how antisemitism is understood and addressed by their learners.

Historian and U.S. Special Envoy to Monitor and Combat Antisemitism, Deborah Lipstadt, pushed back against a lachrymose approach to this issue, saying, "We need to focus on the *joys of being Jewish* and not just the *oys*. Let's put the joy back into the oy!"[214] Since October 7, the phrase, "too much 'oy' and not enough 'joy'" has appeared frequently in Jewish communal discourse.

* * *

Over the past two years, the Anti-Defamation League (ADL) has published studies evaluating colleges in the United States based on how welcoming they are to Jewish students, primarily based on reported antisemitic incidents.[215] Rabbi Ben Berger, Senior Vice President for Jewish Education, Community, and Culture at Hillel International, an organization that fosters Jewish life on campus, told me:

> While the ADL's report brought much-needed attention to the rise in antisemitism on campus, its framing reflected a particular narrative—one that privileges public incidents and institutional responses over the more textured and varied experiences of Jewish students. The letter-grade system, though accessible and media-friendly, flattened complex realities into overly simplistic judgments. It offered little space for the joy, resilience, and vibrant Jewish life that often thrive on campuses even amidst challenging circumstances. More importantly, it failed to capture the nuance of relationships between Jewish students, campus administrators, and Jewish organizations—relationships that are often dynamic, imperfect, and locally shaped. The best way to understand Jewish life on a campus is not through rankings or headlines, but through listening: to students themselves, to the professionals who support them, and to the communal ecosystems they help build. Jewish professionals, in turn, have the opportunity—and the

> responsibility—to present a fuller picture to high school students: one that includes both the "oy" and the "joy."[216]

I believe that strategies like these have merit. I also believe that if we define Jewishness solely based on suffering and persecution, we shouldn't be surprised if Jewish youth and young adults perceive the Jewish world as the source of more "oy" than "joy."

Jewish educators should work to restore balance between "oy" and "joy," but we must also be careful not to overcorrect. In the aftermath of October 7, it is important to acknowledge and teach about Jewish pain and suffering, while also highlighting positive aspects, particularly stories of resilience and heroism. One possible approach for educators is to show how Jewish life can be enhanced even when set against a backdrop of hardship and struggle.

Over the coming years, Jewish educators will face the challenge of balancing emotions when recounting the events of October 7 and their aftermath. One senior Jewish educator I spoke with was adamant that only stories of heroism, resilience, and pride should be shared. Meanwhile, other educators are deep in planning memorial ceremonies for groups visiting the site of the Nova music festival.

For Jewish educators, this could be a guide to our work moving forward. In recent years, many in the Jewish community have embraced the catchy phrase that Jewish life should be "more about the 'joy' than the 'oy.'" Yet, I believe both feelings are essential. The "oy" and the "joy" are equally important parts of Jewish life, and focusing on each enriches the experience of both.

I have long thought that a strong and enduring Jewish identity is fostered by positive *intrinsic* motivations and not by *extrinsic* forces that others impose on us. But I now realize that we must also internalize the tragedies that have befallen our people. In doing so, we recognize that persecution and victimization are inescapable attributes of what it has always meant to be Jewish. If we understand the pain we have endured, we can more deeply appreciate, celebrate, and be proud of who we are as a people.

In the effort to bring more joy into Jewish life and education, the discussion often focuses on fostering pride. Jewish pride should naturally result from Jewish learning, and more joyful Jewish experiences can encourage people to achieve this goal.

I was reminded of this in an unexpected way during my initial meeting with then-ninety-two-year-old Bernie Marcus of the Marcus Foundation. We discussed what ultimately became RootOne, an initiative of The Jewish Education Project to send thousands of Jewish teenagers to Israel on pre-college educational programs.[217] I came with a full PowerPoint deck outlining the core educational objectives of the program: Teenagers needed to know more about Israel, be prepared to stand up for Israel on campus, and develop strong Jewish connections. Bernie listened attentively and then said, "I want Jewish kids to go to college as proud Jews with strong connections to Israel," but added, "don't forget one thing. The kids also need to have fun."

The exchange with Bernie Marcus reminded me of one of my first conversations with Dr. Barry Chazan, who I first met at the Hebrew University in Jerusalem in the mid-1990s. I suggested to Barry that, in addition to his eight characteristics of informal Jewish education, he should consider including "fun."[218] I distinctly remember Barry preferring not to use the term "fun." Instead, he favored the word "engagement." It was Barry's core belief that informal Jewish education is more than just fun. Through a sense of engagement, real joy can be found through a deep connection to the educational experience. I now believe he was right.

This belief in the need for Jewish educators to revive Jewish fun, joy, and pride is based on two assumptions discussed in this book. First, we live in an era of choice, and most Jews today voluntarily participate in Jewish life and education at various stages of their lives.[219] Second, for Jewish identity to be thick and enduring, it needs to be based on positive, internal beliefs, values, and emotions—not external actors.

Rabbi Lord Jonathan Sacks wrote, "Antisemitism is something that happens to Jews; it does not define who we are." He stressed, "Jews are the objects of antisemitism, not its cause.... It can never be the basis of an identity."[220]

Jewish educators are often on the front lines of the struggle against today's antisemitism. However, as discussed previously, identifying and responding to antisemitism is not enough. Jewish educators must work to maintain Jewish joy and Jewish pride in a world where it seems that so many people "just don't like us."

Indeed, for Jewish educators, the pedagogic question of our time could be: *In a time of increased antisemitism and anti-Israel agitation, how do you educate toward greater Jewish pride?*

Some Jewish educators are drawing on analogous models of teaching about "pride" to guide these discussions. They are inspired by the ways both the LGBTQ and Black communities have used pride to strengthen their collective identity and expression. Ben Freeman, a Scottish-born Jewish educator, describes the concept of Jewish pride as particularly powerful, stating,

> Pride teaches us that we have value, and that we should not be treated in the way that we are.

> Jewish pride is the most effective way to fight Jewhate, because it empowers Jews to stand up and fight and to encourage our allies by being able to share our experiences. We should not be afraid to center ourselves in our own stories.[221]

This statement emphasizes the importance of fostering Jewish pride as both an identity and an educational goal. It also provides guidance for Jewish educators facing a generation of learners who experience antisemitism and anti-Israel sentiment differently from those who preceded them. To prepare students for this reality, educators must instill Jewish pride as both a positive alternative and a strong foundation to withstand the growing hostility toward the Jewish people and, by extension, Israel.

One of the primary components of Jewish pride is Jewish knowledge. However, in our current world, knowledge is both critical and critically lacking in many of our conversations. Consequently, some individuals within the Jewish community have advocated for knowledge as the key to boosting Jewish pride. They believe that if Jews gain a deeper understanding of Jewish and Zionist history, they would be more inclined to develop positive attitudes towards their Jewish identity, the Jewish community, and Israel.[222]

Acquiring more knowledge is just one method of pedagogically achieving Jewish pride. Many other pedagogical approaches and experiences can also be highly effective. Watching a Jewish movie, visiting a Jewish site (including but not limited to Israel), listening to Jewish music, eating a Jewish meal, and spending time with Jewish friends are all examples of positive Jewish experiences that can foster greater Jewish pride.

Under the leadership of Dr. Samantha Vinokor-Meinrath at The Jewish Education Project, ways of achieving Jewish pride outcomes are being developed, taught, and field-tested.[223] Among the desired outcomes are Jewish learners developing strong positive self-images as Jews, knowing more about what it means to be Jewish, being able to express Jewishness among diverse people, and seeing themselves as part of the past, present, and future of the Jewish people.

It is interesting to note that the concept of Jewish pride doesn't always translate well. In Hebrew, there are two distinct words for "pride," each carrying very different connotations. *Ga'avah* usually has a negative sense, referring to arrogance, haughtiness, or an inflated ego. In biblical and rabbinic sources, *ga'avah* is often considered a moral failing or even a sin that distances a person from humility and community. By contrast, *Ge'ut* / *Ge'on* carries a positive or aspirational meaning, signifying dignity, majesty, or healthy self-respect.

In the Tanakh, *ge'ut* is used to describe God's greatness, as well as the inner strength and dignity of the Jewish people. It affirms identity, communal pride, resilience, and dignity. It is clearly the latter interpretation of pride that Jewish and Israel education should strive for.

* * *

Antisemitism and Israel, so closely linked today, will likely have the greatest impact on Jewish pride worldwide in the foreseeable future. Israel education will play a critical role in this process.

Israel is always going to be a source of pride for many Jews worldwide. These Jews will continue to visit Israel, marveling at the numerous innovations from the start-up nation, and will always rally for Israel whenever and wherever they can.

There will also be Jews around the world for whom Israel, especially the Israeli government, is not a source of pride, but, at times, a source of shame.

For Israel education to succeed globally, it must emphasize joy and foster a sense of Jewish pride. I recognize that achieving this will be a significant challenge. Some in the Jewish community naturally embrace this perspective, while an increasing number may find it difficult. There will also always be those who view certain Israeli policies or actions as tarnishing the entire Zionist enterprise.

One of my earliest understandings of Zionism was as a movement dedicated to building, maintaining, developing, and improving the Jewish state. For Jewish educators, each of these actions is equally important because Zionism remains an unfinished project that must continually strive to do better. As Jewish educators, I believe this is something we can and should take pride in.

I believe that teaching Jewish pride in response to increasing antisemitism and anti-Israel sentiments will be a significant challenge for Jewish educators in the future. However, simply telling someone to be a proud Jew will not work. Jewish pride must be taught and nurtured through experiences. In some respects, I view this challenge as similar to how we teach young people to love God.

Teaching *Ahavat Yisrael* (a love of Israel) can be an extremely powerful approach. In his book *The Philosophy of Israel Education*, Barry Chazan frames Israel education as a form of engagement in which love is one of several desired outcomes. He presents Israel education as a values-driven process through which students are invited to experience *"knowledge, commitment, belonging, and yes, love—for a real, imperfect, vital Jewish state and people."*[224]

One of the more significant Israel educators in my life, Steve Israel, recounted the following episode:

> On a working trip to New Jersey a few years back, I was invited to speak to an audience of male middle school students at a large prestigious Jewish school. As I was introduced to the students in the large auditorium, the rabbi who was in charge of my visit mentioned that I had come to talk to them about the Israel that they loved. He then went out of the hall (to my relief) and I put aside my prepared talk to engage them in conversation. Is it true they all love Israel? I asked them. They all answered unanimously "yes," and when I probed, they told me that it was school policy to love Israel. I asked how many had been to Israel and a minority said that they had visited. I then asked the majority if they could ever love a girl that they had never seen. Most, emphatically, said "no." So I asked if they did not think it strange that they could love a place they had never seen and when I made it clear that they could really speak their mind and asked them how they really felt about Israel and whether they really loved it, many "broke down" and confessed that these were things they had been taught to say and some said that they felt guilty that they didn't really love Israel the way they were "meant to."[225]

When deconstructing the experience, Steve refers to the notion of *idealism* being a necessary component to incorporate elements of caring and connection. But he also speaks about both criticism and complexity as necessary components in understanding, relating to, and indeed loving the country that Israel is striving to be.

This idea of loving Israel while grappling with its imperfections was popularized in Israel education by Robbie Gringras's use of the phrase "hugging and wrestling."[226] Gringras was quick to point out that the most important word in this phrase is "and." He insisted that educators must cultivate loving connections with Israel, as well as, and often before, confronting its critical challenges and imperfections.

More recently, Rabbi Dr. Laura Novak Winer has questioned whether cultivating *Ahavat Yisrael* is still a useful paradigm in educational settings. She points out that while *love* is often valued, cultivating it is difficult to measure and risks becoming indoctrination. She proposes *"Yediat Yisrael"* (knowing Israel), as a more educationally sound and assessable goal.

To fully understand this concept, a biblical understanding of *yediat* (knowing) is essential. It connotes far more than intellectual or even experiential knowledge. Instead, it often refers to *intimate* knowledge of something, such as God or a sexual partner. Winer believes that education should seek to cultivate this sense of knowing by fostering connections and relationships. She states, *"You first have to know it. Yediat Yisrael may lead to Ahavat Yisrael, but that is not the primary objective."*[227]

Earlier in this book, I referenced Dr. Mijal Bitton's essay in which she contends that the visceral experience of collective suffering—such as the shock and grief following the October 7 attacks—creates what she calls Jewish peoplehood: "This is what Jewish peoplehood feels like."[228] Later, in a Substack reflection on a hostage release, she shifted tone to emphasize that joy is an expression of this same communal bond: the elation of "our brothers being home" becomes another dimension of peoplehood.[229]

All these thinkers suggest that Jewish peoplehood is not only born of shared pain but also of shared joy and responsibility.

Post-October 7, the success of Israel education will depend on understanding that we need more "joys" than "oys" in Jewish life. However, there must be more to being Jewish than episodic moments of despair and elation. Only a *sustained* sense of joy, or at least contentment with being Jewish, will ensure that Jewish pride becomes pervasive and, for many, inextricably linked to their relationship with Israel.

Questions to Consider

- Are you optimistic or pessimistic about the future of the Jewish people?
- How do you ensure that moments of Jewish joy and pride are a regular part of your life?

CONCLUSION

The Heroism and Hope of Israel Education

Over the course of my recent sabbatical, I was fortunate enough to be introduced to Theory U. This is a framework developed to bring about change within complex systems by moving individuals and organizations from their present state to an imagined future.[230] This afforded me the opportunity to consider the future of Israel education.

Theory U examines the barriers to change at individual, organizational, and systems levels. Even education, a field frequently tasked with transforming individuals and the world, often struggles to implement necessary changes.

The Theory U framework outlines various reasons why change is so hard to implement. One reason is that people find it difficult to envision an imagined future. At the same time, there is often little incentive for educators to go outside their comfort zones, take risks, and experiment. In many cases, the institutions for which educators work, even though they might declare themselves champions of transformation, are resistant to real change.[231]

Theory U also identifies *emotional resistance* as a key inhibitor of change. Fear and uncertainty often paralyze people or force them to retreat into doing things the way they have always been done.

After October 7, the Jewish community around the world retreated. They did not retreat externally, in that there were widespread demonstrations of support in many forms. Driven by fear, insecurity, and a sense of vulnerability and isolation, it retreated on a collective emotional level. Jewish educators, even if they intellectually believe in a new vision of Israel education, will be unable to realize it unless they can break through this emotional resistance.

This book seeks to outline a vision for the future of Israel education. However, this concluding chapter is specifically designed to inspire educators and those passionate about education. It seeks to provide a call to action, a charge, and a recharging. It's designed to encourage educators to overcome the internal emotional barriers that may be preventing them from reaching their educational goals.

By emphasizing heroism and hope, my goal is to instill in educators the confidence that they are uniquely equipped to implement the changes we so desperately need. Additionally, I want to convey a clear message to all stakeholders in Jewish education, urging them to support educators in achieving these goals.

* * *

Heroism and Israel Education

Since October 7, I have been to Ofakim,[232] a town in southern Israel, several times. I am embarrassed to say that I had never been there before October 7. On one of my first visits, I was struck by a mural prominently displayed in the city center. It showed a female policewoman shaking hands with an Orthodox man. Below was the slogan *Ir Shel Giborim*, "City of Heroes." It was a powerful reminder of the resilience of Ofakim, which faced unspeakable tragedy on October 7.[233]

Photo by David Bryfman

It is important to note that, prior to October 7, the town motto of Ofakim was *Ir Shel Anashim*, "City of People." The transformation of "people" to "heroes" tells you something about the people who live there.

It is important to note that, on my trips to Ofakim, I met with many incredibly impressive women, particularly in the education sector. A large number of them performed critical roles during and after the October 7 attacks. All of them were quick to point out that now the true motto of Ofakim is *Ir shel giborim ve'giborot*. Because the Hebrew language is gendered, this means "city of male heroes and female heroes." When we discuss the changes needed in Jewish and Israel education, fields predominantly composed of women, I cannot help but think of the story of female heroism.

Heroes are often defined as people who put other people's lives before their own. The people of southern Israel are certainly heroes. The south is filled with hundreds of stories of heroism. They include stories of educators who often put the needs of their students ahead of their own personal and family needs in the aftermath of October 7 without hesitating.

Without minimizing the actions of these Israelis, we should note that the term "hero" has been applied to other educators in other contexts in recent years. For example, during the Covid pandemic, when educators—and numerous others—often risked their lives to keep society functioning.

I am more than comfortable and extremely grateful to acknowledge that there are different shapes and sizes of heroism in this world, and we need more of it.

Among the heroes who prioritized others' needs were the thousands of Jewish educators worldwide who sprang into action after October 7. They addressed the emotional and intellectual needs of their students and families, often sacrificing their own well-being in doing so. These educators worked tirelessly during those incredibly tense and emotional days and, if they hadn't already, quickly became role models for our children and their families.

This book begins by emphasizing that, to be the most effective educators they can be, Jewish educators must prioritize their personal well-being and their relationship with Israel before engaging with their students. It concludes by recognizing that it may be in the DNA of educators to do the opposite. They choose to be heroes who put their learners' needs first.

Let us all strive to achieve the correct balance between well-being and heroism. Let us also ensure that we recognize, praise, and value our Jewish educators for all that they do each and every day; especially when the times demand that they go above and beyond their regular duties.

* * *

Hope and Israel Education

The final and enduring message I want to leave you with is this: education has always been, and must remain, a source of hope. Teachers and educators should approach their work with the goal of improving individual lives, strengthening communities, and making the world a better place.

Educators must always be optimistic. As educational pioneer John Dewey said, "Optimism is an essential ingredient of effective thinking. Without it, thought is inhibited at the outset."[234] But hope is not the same as optimism. As Rabbi Lord Jonathan Sacks stated, "Optimism is the belief that things will get better. Hope is the belief that, if we work hard enough, together we can make things better."[235]

There is also the question of faith. Hope and faith are distinct concepts, and Jewish educators should recognize this important difference. Faith often provides more certainty than hope, while hope allows for greater human agency. This topic demands a deep theological discussion, which Jewish educators should facilitate with their students.

In a post-October 7 world, hope might be Israel education's most powerful tool. Jewish educators must pursue a better world in which Jewish learners can actively participate in creating a better future.

One of our duties as Israel educators must be to empower our learners to see themselves as active players in the Jewish story. A story about, in the words of Israel's national anthem, the quest "to be a free people, in the land of Zion and Jerusalem."

Mandating hope in Israel education does not mean ignoring imperfections or believing that hope alone will fix things. Hope acknowledges that October 7 is not merely a blip in Jewish and Israeli history, but a pivotal moment that demands we begin to construct a brighter future. Jewish educators have the dual duty of addressing current needs and preparing for a better tomorrow. This hope also serves as a reminder of the significant impact education can have around the world.

* * *

A Final Reflection

Before I say my final words on this subject, I present a reflection from my journal after my first visit to the Nova Festival massacre site in December 2023.

Eucalyptus Trees in Re'im

Nothing could be more beautiful, and nothing could be more paradoxical for me, than an Australian, living in New York, coming to Israel 116 days after October 7, and standing in a field filled with eucalyptus trees.

And the kalaniyot. I don't know how to translate "kalaniyot" and the truth is that I don't want to.[236] They are the red flowers that bloom in Israel, often after the winter rains come and are a signal for all that spring is coming.

But amongst these eucalyptus trees and the kalaniyot is death.

Thousands who danced here and hundreds who were slaughtered here.

Some of those who danced still live, or so we hope, because something inside each of them has also died too.[237]

One day, hopefully sooner rather than later, we will be able to dance again,

Until then I will never look at eucalyptus trees and kalaniyot in the same way.

We will, we must dance again.

In the months after October 7, and even to this day, posters and bumper stickers can be found in Israel and around the world with the slogan, "We Will Dance Again."

In the days and weeks after October 7, when Jewish educators were scrambling with what to teach and how to teach about that horrific day, Dr. Shelley Kedar of The Jewish Agency, would say to me and my colleagues, "Just teach them Nova."

Clearly, Shelley knew then, as we all do now, that October 7 was much more than just the slaughter of 378 people and the capture of forty-four hostages from the site of the Nova music festival in the fields of Kibbutz Re'im. But Shelley also knew then, as we all do now, that imagery, symbols, metaphors, stories, young faces, evil and heroism, and so many other things did and will continue to matter for Jewish educators in a post-October 7 world.

One of the most important slogans to emerge after October 7 for educators is "We will dance again." It is not just a slogan for Israelis, but also a slogan for Jews around the world. It is not just a slogan filled with spirit and resilience, but also with hope. The hope that we will indeed dance again is one that we, as Jewish educators, have an obligation to embrace. It is our sacred duty to do so.

And the greatest hope of them all:

אני מבטיח לך, ילדה שלי קטנה
שזאת תהיה המלחמה האחרונה
Ani mavtiyach lach, yaldah sheli katanah.
Shezot ti'hyeh hamilchamah ha'acharonah
I promise you, my daughter,
that this will be the last war[238]

EPILOGUE

The first draft of this epilogue was written on October 13, 2025, Erev Simchat Torah 5786. It was 738 days after October 7, 2023.

The last living hostages from Gaza had been returned to their families. Twenty-one dead hostages remained in Gaza.

American President Donald Trump had returned to the United States following rapturous applause in Israel and the 2025 peace summit in Egypt. I will leave it to others to debate whether he achieved a ceasefire or a peace process.

Today, despite mixed emotions and unrealized objectives, Israelis and Jews worldwide are not only breathing again but celebrating and dancing again. They are joyful at what is being recognized as the end to the longest war in Israel's seventy-eight-year history. Then, events like those at Bondi Beach hit us hard—yet again. Perhaps this is the eternal plight of the Jewish people and the Jewish educator. But even in the face of tragedy, I continue to implore educators to remain educators:

As educators, teachers, and parents, our first obligation is to listen to our children. To all their emotions: fear, anger, confusion, and sadness. Sometimes telling children to "be proud," to "go outside and shine your menorah brightly," is not the right response in the immediate aftermath of violence. Sometimes the most Jewish thing we can do is sit quietly with them in their fear. To be scared together for a moment. Emotions are real, and they cannot always be controlled or overridden by ideology or slogans.

Adults can be adults. But we must also let kids be kids.

It is too soon to know what the long-term implications of all this will be for Israel and the Jewish people. As noted throughout this book, many of the issues that have been grappled with in these pages existed before October 7 and will remain with us.

Up to now, I have been hesitant to reiterate a sentiment that appears in the preface of this book. But now, in the aftermath of October 7 and the war that followed, I feel more deeply than ever that if the Shoah and the establishment of the State of Israel were the defining moments of Jewish civilization in the twentieth century, then I do not think it too far-fetched to posit that October 7 and its aftermath will define what Jewish life will look like in the twenty-first century and perhaps beyond.

But no matter what, we, the Jewish people and this audience of Jewish educators, cannot return to business as usual. We cannot go back to the way things were on October 6, 2023. We cannot pretend that things were perfect then. We cannot continue our collective work as if the last two years were a mere blip in time.

In a recent article, Michael Koplow, of the Israel Policy Forum, is quoted as saying:

> American Jewish institutions are going to have to grapple with what it means for American Jews to have a different relationship with Israel. And that's going to impact all sorts of things. It's going to impact funding. It's going to impact

> American Jewish education on Israel. It's going to impact the types of Israeli organizations that American Jews interact with. So, it's way, way too early to say anything definitively, but I don't think that we should expect that now that the war is over, everything is going to just go back to the status quo ante, as if the last two years didn't happen.[239]

There is a debate going on today in the Jewish world, a true *machloket le shem shamayim*, an argument in the name of heaven: There are those in the Jewish community who are suggesting that it is now time to remove our yellow ribbons and dog tags inscribed with "Bring them home now"—reminders of the plight of the hostages.

Rabbi Menachem Creditor of UJA Federation New York proposed in a Facebook post that we might consider burying these sacred objects. He even provided a prayer for conducting such a ritual:

A Prayer for Burying "Bring Them Home Now" Dog Tags[240]
Mekor HaChayim, Source of all Life,
We stand today with trembling hearts,
bearing these small pieces of metal—
once cold, now warmed by years of tears
and hope and holy sweat.

For two years, these dog tags rested upon our hearts,
carrying our brothers and sisters,
our children and elders,
whose faces we carried into every prayer,
every dream, every moment of waiting.

We wore them as shields of faith,
as promises never to forget.
Each clink and gleam was a heartbeat of Am Yisrael,
a whispered "Bring them home. Now."

Now, as we return these amulets to the earth,
we do not discard them.
We lay them gently, as we would lay a loved one,
trusting that memory is eternal,
that love does not rust,
that sanctity can dwell in metal, in tears, in time.

Holy One, let this burial be a bridge—
from pain to promise,
from captivity to compassion,
from symbol to action.

May the ground receive these sacred tokens
as we continue to carry their spirit in our souls.
May every name engraved here
shine in the heavens as a light that can never be extinguished.

And may the world never again need such amulets,
for all Your children to be free,
safe in their homes,
whole in their hearts,
together in peace.

Amen.

Others in the Jewish community have been equally outspoken in suggesting that these symbols should not be removed until the very last hostage body is returned to Israel. This message is amplified by an official statement of the Hostages and Missing

Families Forum, an organization representing the families of captives. They said, "Our struggle is not over. It will not end until the last hostage is located and returned for proper burial."[241]

As is often the case in an argument in the name of heaven, there is no wrong response to this disagreement other than a process that does not ensure that *eilu v'eilu*, "these and those" voices, are expressed and heard.

I believe that as of the conclusion of Simchat Torah 5786, Jewish education, with Israel integral to it in every possible way, begins a new chapter. The past two years have been brutal and today must be viewed as a new beginning.

The tendency might be for Jewish educators to return as quickly as they can to October 6. Instead, today must be the day that Jewish educators declare that they are forever changed. A day when we can collectively declare that we are moving from a defensive posture to a proactive one.

Our primary task is not to help our learners combat the negative forces in this world, but to instill in them the knowledge, skills, and dispositions that will allow them to be proud and empowered Jews and global citizens. The hardships of October 7 and its aftermath took a huge toll on the entire Jewish people. Jewish educators now have the enormous responsibility of helping to rebuild a generation. We can only do so if we confront the new realities in which we live.

With the ceasefire declared and the Gaza war officially ended, this book serves as something like a marker in time, reflecting the challenges Jewish educators worldwide have faced over the past two years. My humble hope is that the questions and issues it raises will act as a blueprint for the essential conversations that Jewish educators—and all stakeholders in Jewish and Israel education—must engage in today, and in the months and years to come.

An Addendum to an Epilogue

It is January 26, 2026, and it is now really over. It is difficult to call today a day of joy, but it is certainly one of relief and we can finally exhale. The body of Ran Gvili, the last remaining deceased hostage, has been returned to Israel, 843 days after October 7, 2023.

With the final deceased hostage returned to Israel, UJA Federation of New York, together with the Hostage and Missing Families Forum, announced a campaign to collect hostage tags and yellow ribbons from the public to make a communal commemorative piece of artwork to symbolize the end of this moment in Jewish time. Tomorrow, I return to my office, and I will remove the count-up clock that has been with me for every one of those 843 days.

It is strange that we as a Jewish people treat the return of a dead body with so much reverence and even celebration—but that is a lesson for another day.

APPENDIX A

Lesson Plan/Activity (*Peulah*) Based on Rav Kook's Jewish Identity Triangle

Grade/Group: Middle school, high school, or adult learners
Time: 45–75 minutes
Materials: Large drawing of Rabbi Kook's Jewish identity triangle (on board or poster paper, or even marked out on the floor for people to stand on), markers, individual copies of the triangle (optional).

Core Learning Objectives

1. Students will be able to explain the three dimensions of Rabbi Kook's Jewish identity triangle (Torat Yisrael, Am Yisrael, Eretz Yisrael) and identify characteristics associated with each.

2. Students will reflect on their own Jewish identity and place themselves on the triangle, articulating how their lived experiences shape their connection to Judaism.
3. *(Optional extension objective for educator groups)*: Participants will understand their role in helping learners explore all dimensions of Jewish identity and consider how educational experiences can influence identity development over time.

Lesson Sequence

1. Introduction (5 minutes)

- Display the triangle.
- Introduce the idea that Jewish identity is multidimensional and dynamic.
- Explain that Rabbi Kook used this model to describe different ways Jews connect to their Jewishness.

2. Teaching the Three Corners (10–15 minutes)

Using clear language and relatable examples, describe each corner:

Torat Yisrael (The Torah / Tradition Corner)

- Represents Jewish values, texts, rituals, and religious life.
- People in this corner connect through learning, observance, synagogue life, Shabbat, and Jewish ritual.

Am Yisrael (The Jewish People Corner)

- Represents cultural connection, community, shared celebration, and belonging.
- People in this corner feel most Jewish when among other Jews—at holidays and cultural events, or during Jewish travel.

Eretz Yisrael (The Land / Israel Corner)

- Represents the connection to the Land and State of Israel.
- People in this corner may travel to Israel, follow Israeli news, support Israeli institutions, or feel Israel is central to their Jewish life.

Encourage learners to notice that people can express identity differently and that no single approach is "more authentic" or "better" than another.

3. Personal Reflection Activity (10–15 minutes)

- Invite participants to approach the large triangle.
- Ask them to *place their initials* anywhere inside it to represent where they see their Jewish identity *today*.
- Allow time for hesitation—it's part of the process. Eventually one person will begin and others will follow.

4. Sharing Reflections (10–20 minutes)

- One by one, participants briefly explain why they placed themselves where they did.
- Encourage listening with respect, curiosity, and no judgment.

- The facilitator models reflective language and validates multiple experiences.

5. Identity as Journey (10 minutes)

- Ask participants to return to their initials and draw two arrows:

1. An arrow pointing toward their initials: Where they came from (e.g., upbringing, personal history, their community).
2. An arrow pointing away from their initials: Where they hope to move in their Jewish life (no timeframe attached).

- Discuss:
- *"Identity is not fixed; it evolves. Our relationship to Torah, People, and Israel can grow and shift over time."*

6. Closing Reflection (5 minutes)

For Students:

- "What is one new perspective you gained about Jewish identity today?"

For Educators:

- Add the educator lens:
- *"Our role is to help learners explore the full triangle. When someone expands their identity as a result of educational experience, that is transformative education."*

Assessment / Evidence of Learning

- Observation of thoughtful placement and explanation on the triangle.
- Participation in group discussion and reflection.
- (Optional) Written reflection on identity "journeys."

After drawing Rabbi Kook's triangle, I continue to describe the three dimensions of his theory, taking liberties as educators do, to make the source relevant for today's learners:

> Torat Yisrael is the corner that represents the Jewish values, texts, and wisdom that connect people to their Jewish selves. You all know people who reside predominantly in this corner of the triangle. Stereotypically, they are very religious, in your minds they might be ultra-Orthodox and notice if the image you conjured up is of a man. But you also probably know other non-Orthodox religious Jews who also define their connection to being Jewish through Torah and Torah values. They too attend synagogue or Temple frequently, celebrate Shabbat, and keep kosher to some degree, because it is the laws and values of Torah that shape their lives.
>
> Am Yisrael is the corner of the triangle for Jews who just love being around other Jews. You know these folks too. They never miss a Jewish book or film festival; they love eating Jewish foods; and they participate in almost every celebration of Jewish life they can get to. You might also notice these Jews when they travel, always searching out Jewish sites and communities anywhere in the world they travel. For these Jews, belonging to the Jewish

> people fills them with joy and pride, but after tragedies, sometimes with complete sadness.
>
> The Eretz Yisrael corner is for the Zionists. But it's not just for the ones who decide to live their lives in Israel. It's also for the Jews for whom Israel is almost everything. They've likely traveled to Israel before, likely attended an Israel-focused summer camp or youth movement, give money to Israeli causes, and have the *Jerusalem Post* or *Haaretz* as their browser home page. For these Jews, Israel is central to their core being even if they don't actually live there—yet.

Then the activity moves into the active stage:

> Very few people find themselves in one corner of the triangle. Most people who have some sort of connection with their Jewish self feel it is connected to at least two, if not all three.
>
> So, follow these instructions carefully…
>
> Approach the triangle and place your initials where you see your Jewish identity today.

Invariably the audience hesitates until one person starts and the rest follow:

> Now explain to the group why you decided to put yourself where you did on the triangle.

After a while, everyone in the group has hopefully had a chance to speak:

> I now want you to go to your initials and draw two arrows. The first is an arrow pointing to your initials, indicating where you have come from. The second is an arrow departing from your initials, indicating where you would like to move to.

I deliberately put no time frame on when learners decide to start or end their journey, but the point is then made very clearly: "Identity is not a stagnant construct, it is constantly altering and changing—it is a journey."[242]

If I am working with a group of educators, I might add the following:

> As an educator, it is your responsibility to help people consider all aspects of the triangle, encouraging them to explore and experiment with different corners of the triangle. When someone claims to have changed their position as a result of the educational experience, that is what is known as "transformative education"—something many of us strive for.

NOTES

Introduction

1 Arendt, H, "The Crisis in Education" in *Between Past and Future: Eight Exercises in Political Thought*, Viking Press, 1954.

2 Kurtzer Y. and Winer, L.N., panelists, *ReCHARGING Reform Judaism: New paradigms for Jewish education (Plenum IV)*, "New paradigms for Israel education" moderated by Kaiserman, S., The Jewish Broadcasting Service, posted July 26, 2024, https://www.youtube.com/watch?v=n-YrIK8Nlv0.

3 Katznelson, Berl, and Ben Halpern, ed., *Selected Writings* (Histadrut, 1956).

4 Bryfman, D., "A new Anne Frank moment," *The Times of Israel – The Blogs*, December 13, 2023, https://blogs.timesofisrael.com/a-new-anne-frank-moment/.

5 Zohar Raviv. "The issue is not "the issues," but the spiraling collapse in our ability to discuss them." *eJewish Philanthropy*, June 1, 2021, https://ejewishphilanthropy.com/the-issue-is-not-the-issues-but-the-spiraling-collapse-in-our-ability-to-discuss-them/.

6 Lanski, A., "Your daily Phil: Anne Lanski on Israel education beyond mifgash, Jewish groups prep for Massachusetts ethnic studies push," *eJewish Philanthropy*, October 3, 2023, https://ejewishphilanthropy.com/your-daily-phil-anne-lanski-on-israel-education-beyond-mifgash-jewish-groups-prep-for-massachusetts-ethnic-studies-push/.

7 Korczak, J. as cited in Goldberg, A., *Janusz Korczak: The man and his mission* (Feldheim Publishers, 2000).

Section One

8 Heschel, A. J., *I asked for wonder: A spiritual anthology,* ed., S. H. Dresner (Crossroad Publishing, 1997), 18.

Chapter One

9 CAJE is the Coalition for the Advancement of Jewish Education.

10 Palmer, P. J., *The Courage to Teach: Exploring the inner landscape of a teacher's life* (JosseyBass, 2007), xi.

11 Palmer, P. J., *The Courage to Teach: Exploring the inner landscape of a teacher's life* (JosseyBass, 2007), 11.

12 Bryfman, D., "Jewish educators have nightmares about Oct. 7," *eJewish Philanthropy*, March 20, 2024, https://ejewishphilanthropy.com/jewish-educators-have-dreams-about-oct-7/.

13 The *"matzav"* refers to the situation in Israel regarding the broader security, political, and emotional reality surrounding the Israeli-Palestinian conflict, specifically tensions, wars, or general instability.

14 "Barriers to Entry: Exploring Educator Reticence for Engaging with the Israeli–Palestinian Conflict," featured in *Teaching Israel: Studies of Pedagogy from the Field* (Brandeis University Press, 2024).

15 Zakai, S., *My second-favorite country: How American Jewish children think about Israel* (Rutgers University Press, 2009).

16 Palmer, Parker, "The Heart of a Teacher," *Change Magazine* 29, no. 6, 1997, 14–21.

17 Bryfman, D., "Educators are real people too," *eJewish Philanthropy,* July 18, 2014, https://ejewishphilanthropy.com/educators-are-real-people-too/.

Chapter Two

18 "The threefold bond that unites our nation—the Torah, the Land of Israel, and the nation itself—is one entity. Separation between these elements causes the destruction of all. Only the union of all three can bring true redemption. A love of Torah without a love of the nation and the Land, or a love of the nation without the Torah and the Land, or a love of the Land without the Torah and the nation—each of these is a dismembered love, destined to wither. Only their unified appearance gives them life, strength, and holiness." From

Kook, A. I., *Orot Yisrael (Lights of Israel)*, trans. B. Naor, 2015 (Jerusalem: Kodesh Press, 1920), Sections 1–6 and 18–19.

19 Grant, L. D. and Kopelowitz, E. M., *Israel Education Matters: A 21st Century Paradigm for Jewish Education* (Center for Jewish Peoplehood Education, 2012).

20 Benjamin (Bibi) Netanyahu has been the Prime Minister of Israel from 2009–2021 and again from 2022 until the present time. (In between there were too short Prime Minister terms of Naftali Bennett (June 2021–June 22) and Yair Lapid (July 2022–December 2022).

21 The Ministry of Diaspora Affairs and Combatting Antisemitism created both UnitEd, specifically to work with formal Jewish educational institutions, and Mosaic United to work with informal educational experiences throughout the Jewish world.

22 Bennett, N., "Why Israel is investing in Diaspora Jewish education," *Jewish Telegraphic Agency,* April 26, 2018, https://www.jta.org/2018/04/26/united-states/israel-investing-diaspora-jewish-education. Although not everyone agrees with this sentiment as expressed by Fleischmann, I., "Israelis shouldn't fund Diaspora Jews," *Israel Hayom*, July 21, 2020, https://www.israelhayom.com/opinions/israelis-shouldnt-fund-diaspora-jews/.

23 Bitton, M., "That Pain You're Feeling Is Peoplehood," *SAPIR Journal*, November 1, 2023, https://sapirjournal.org/war-in-israel/2023/that-pain-youre-feeling-is-peoplehood/.

Chapter Three

24 Aish, "Ben Zussman's final letter to his family," *Aish*, January 7, 2024, https://aish.com/ben-zussmans-final-letter-to-his-family/.

25 For full video of Sarit Zussman including educational framing and discussion questions, Rabbi Benji Levy interview with Sarit Zussman, *Rabbi Levy,* 2024, https://www.rabbibenji.com/saritzussman.

26 These dates refer to significant wars and conflicts in Israel's history—1948: The War of Independence; 1956: The Sinai War; 1967: The Six Day War; 1973: The Yom Kippur War; 1982: The

Lebanon War; 1987: The First Intifada; 2000: The Second Intifada; 2006: The Second Lebanon War.

27 Some examples include Matar, H., "How October 7 has changed us all — and what it signals for our struggle," *+972 Magazine*, November 8, 2023, https://www.972mag.comZuxxman/october-war-israelis-palestinians-historic/.

28 Yerushalmi, Y. H., *Zakhor: Jewish history and Jewish memory* (University of Washington Press, 1982), 42–43.

29 Sacks, J. L., "Acceptance Address at the 2013 Templeton Prize ceremony," *Templeton Prize*, May 2013, https://www.templetonprize.org/laureate-sub/sacks-acceptance-address/.

30 Infeld, Avraham, *A Passion for a People: Lessons from the Life of a Jewish Educator* (Jerusalem: Melitz, 2017).

31 Halbwachs, M., *On collective memory*, trans. L. A. Coser (University of Chicago Press, 1980).

32 Wertsch, J. V., *Voices of collective remembering* (Cambridge University Press, 2002), 67.

33 Assmann, A., *Cultural memory and Western civilization: Functions, media, archives* (Cambridge University Press, 2011), 132.

34 Jacobs, B. M., "Teaching and learning Jewish history in the 21st century: New priorities and opportunities," *Journal of Jewish Education* 84, no. 2 (2018), 148–176.

35 Raviv, Z. "Beyond 'Never Again': Returning to identity in Jewish, Israeli, and Zionist education," *The Jerusalem Post.* March 30, 2025, https://www.jpost.com/opinion/article-848145.

36 Raviv, Z. "The story of the ever-living people." *The Lookstein Center for Jewish Education*, September 24, 2024, https://www.lookstein.org/journal-article/f_24/the-story-of-the-ever-living-people/ and Raviv, Z. "Beyond "Never Again": Returning to identity in Jewish, Israeli, and Zionist education." *The Jerusalem Post,* March 30, 2025, https://www.jpost.com/opinion/article-848145.

37 Blas H. "Teaching Israel in the wake of October 7," *The Jerusalem Post*, February 17, 2024, https://www.jpost.com/israel-news/article-787212.

38 Zion, N., & Dishon, D. *A different night: The family participation haggadah*. (Shalom Hartman Institute, 1997), p. 17.

39 Meltzer, Z., "Story bearers needed," *The Times of Israel,* October 22, 2021, https://blogs.timesofisrael.com/story-bearers-needed/.

Chapter Four

40 Golden, J., "The HeartHeadHand of Israel Education," *Shalom Hartman Institute*, February 1, 2023, https://www.hartman.org.il/remembering-oct-7-with-our-hearts-heads-and-hands/.

41 ibid.

42 Two such examples are Jewish Theological Seminary, *Jewish Day School Standards and Benchmarks*, The Jewish Theological Seminar and Hadar Institute, 2025.

Tefillah standards: Building fluency in Jewish prayer, Hadar, https://www.hadar.org/torah-tefillah/fluency-standards.

43 Founded in 2021 Boundless is a nonprofit think-action tank co-founded by Aviva Klompas and Rachel Fish, focused on revitalizing Israel education and combating Jew-hatred.

44 Boundless and BSG, "Views on Israel and Jewish identity," *Boundless,* August 2024, https://boundlessisrael.org/August%202024%20Examining%20Views%20on%20Israel%20and%20Jewish%20Identity.pdf.

45 Himmelfarb, H. S., "The measurement of Jewish identity," *Journal for the Scientific Study of Religion* 19, no. 1, (1980): 38–52, https://doi.org/10.2307/1386070.

46 Chazan, B. I., *A philosophy of Israel education: A relational approach* (Palgrave Macmillan, 2016).

47 Bryfman, D., "A canon for Israel education," *eJewishPhilanthropy,* September 5, 2024, https://ejewishphilanthropy.com/a-canon-of-jewish-education/.

48 Golden, J., "Jewish power, Jewish vulnerability, and this moment for Israel and the Jewish people," *Shalom Hartman Institute,* November 16, 2023, https://www.hartman.org.il/jewish-power-jewish-vulnerability-and-this-moment-for-israel-and-the-jewish-people/.

49 Jacobs, B. M. and Chazan, B., "18x18 educational dimensions for Jewish life," *Institute for Experiential Jewish Education*, 2018, https://ieje.org/wp-content/uploads/2023/06/18x18-Framework.pdf.

50 Hadar Institute, "Devash: Parashat Lekh Lekha 5786," *Hadar*, 2025, https://www.hadar.org/torah-tefillah/resources/devash-parashat-lekh-lekha-5786/.

51 Center for Israel Education, "Resources for teaching about Passover in Israel," *Center for Israel Education,* https://israeled.org/resources-for-teaching-about-passover-in-israel/.

52 IsraelLINK, "Free lesson or resource (Free/3)," *IsraelLINK,* https://go.israellink.org/free/3/.

53 Jewish LearningWorks, "On the Map: Israel education resource," *Jewish LearningWorks*, 2025. https://jewishlearning.works/israel-education/on-the-map/.

54 "Naomi Shemer (1930–2004)," National Library of Israel, effective March11,2026,https://education-en.nli.org.il/time-capsule/naomi-shemer-1930-2004/.

55 The iCenter and Israel Democracy Institute, "Module 1: Israel and the United States: A Tale of Two Democracies," *For the Sake of Justice*, https://idi.theicenter.org/module-1-israel-and-united-states-tale-two-democracies/index.html.

56 Unpacked for Educators, "The Law of Return [Video]," *Unpacked for Educators*, https://unpacked.education/video/the-law-of-return/.

57 Troy, G., *The Zionist ideas: Visions for the Jewish homeland—then, now, tomorrow*, (Jewish Publication Society/The University of Nebraska Press, 2018).

58 Institute for Curriculum Services, "Maps," *Institute for Curriculum Services*, April 13, 2024, https://icsresources.org/curriculum/maps/.

59 Gringras, R., "Stories For the Sake of Argument: Why The Heck Should I Vote?," https://cdn.prod.website-files.com/61dea925d23bc1bcabf130e9/63a1b35c0638b1efcbe21e59_Why%20The%20Heck%20Should%20I%20Vote_.pdf.

60 Toran, V., "Israeli Arts and Culture: The Ability to Engage," *The Aleph Bet of Israel Education* 2, *The iCenter*, 2021, https://theicenter.org/aleph_bet/israeli-arts-and-culture-the-ability-to-engage/.

61 The Nakba (also spelled Naqba) is an Arabic word meaning "catastrophe" or "disaster." It refers specifically to the mass displacement and dispossession of Palestinians that occurred around the time of the establishment of the State of Israel in 1948.

62 Deir Yassin was a Palestinian Arab village near Jerusalem where, in 1948, it is claimed by some that a massacre by Zionist paramilitary groups resulted in the deaths of over 100 villagers, thus becoming a pivotal and tragic event in the Israeli-Palestinian conflict.

63 The Sabra and Shatila massacre was a 1982 atrocity in which Lebanese Christian militias, with the Israeli military's indirect involvement, killed hundreds to thousands of Palestinian refugees in Beirut's Sabra and Shatila refugee camps.

64 Weiss, S., "The Jews Lied to Me at Summer Camp!," *Tablet Magazine,* May 21, 2021, https://www.tabletmag.com/sections/news/articles/the-jews-lied-to-me-at-summer-camp.

65 "Zionism," *Wikipedia, The Free Encyclopedia*, last modified March 11, 2026, https://en.wikipedia.org/wiki/Zionism.

66 Beaumont-Thomas, B., "Dua Lipa denounces 'Israeli genocide' in Instagram post," *The Guardian*, May 29, 2024, https://www.theguardian.com/music/article/2024/may/29/dua-lipa-denounces-israeli-genocide-in-instagram-post.

67 "Generating Hate: AntiJewish and AntiIsrael Bias in Leading Large Language Models," *AntiDefamation League*, March 20, 2025, https://www.adl.org/resources/report/generating-hate-anti-jewish-and-anti-israel-bias-leading-large-language-models?utm_campaign=asbrief2025&utm_content=e20250327&utm_medium=email&utm_source=whole.

68 Kazenwadel, D. and Steinert, C. V., "How user language affects conflict fatality estimates in ChatGPT," *Journal of Peace Research*, November 3, 2024, https://doi.org/10.1177/00223433241279381.

69 Raviv, Z., "Navigating the age of informed ignorance with Dr. Zohar Raviv," *Cape Jewish Chronicle*, July 1, 2021, https://cjc.org.za/2021/07/01/navigating-the-age-of-informed-ignorance-with-dr-zohar-raviv/.

Chapter Five

70 Levites, A. and Sayfan, L., *GenZ now: Understanding and connecting with Jewish teens today* (The Jewish Education Project; Rosov Consulting, 2019).

71 Genesis 1:27, *Tanakh: The Holy Scriptures* (JPS, 1985).

72 Mizrahi Jews are Jews whose ancestry traces primarily to Middle Eastern and North African countries, including Iraq, Iran, Yemen, Syria, Egypt, Morocco, and Tunisia, among others—of which have histories of persecuting and expelling their Jewish populations in the 1950s.

73 A stipulative definition is a term from the disciplines of philosophy and logic, meaning that you assign a specific definition to a term so the discussion can proceed without confusion.

74 "Working definition of antisemitism," *International Holocaust Remembrance Alliance*, 2016, https://www.holocaustremembrance.com/resources/working-definitions-charters/working-definition-antisemitism.

75 "Working definition of antisemitism," *International Holocaust Remembrance Alliance.*

76 "Jerusalem Declaration on Antisemitism," *Jerusalem Declaration on Antisemitism (JDA), 2021*, https://jerusalemdeclaration.org/wp-content/uploads/JDA-English.pdf.

77 IHRA definition.

78 "What Anti-Israel, Anti-Semitic & Anti-Zionist mean," *Anti-Defamation League*, 2024, https://extremismterms.adl.org/resources/tools-and-strategies/what-anti-israel-anti-semitic-anti-zionist.

79 "Campus antisemitism: A survey of Jewish students in the U.S.," *Anti-Defamation League*, 2023, https://www.adl.org/resources/report/campus-antisemitism-study-campus-climate-and-after-hamas-terrorist-attacks.

80 Various articles from multiple sources discuss this concept, such as:

"Protesters regret 'from the river to the sea' chant upon learning meaning," *Newsweek*, November 15, 2023, https://www.newsweek.com/college-students-protesters-middle-east-gaza-conflict-ignorance-israel-palestine-1860049.

"US students ignorant of slogan's meaning," *Vision Christian Media*, November 20, 2023, https://vision.org.au/read/news/us/us-students-ignorant-of-slogans-meaning/.

81 Kelner, S., "American antizionism," *Sources: A Journal of Jewish Ideas*, 2025, https://www.sourcesjournal.org/articles/american-antizionism?utm_source=chatgpt.com.

82 Sharansky, N., "3D test of anti-Semitism: Demonization, double standards, delegitimization," *Jerusalem Center for Public Affairs*, October 21, 2004, https://jcfa.org/article/3d-test-of-anti-semitism-demonization-double-standards-delegitimization/.

83 Clark, K., "Interpreting Egypt's antisemitic cartoons," *BBC News*, August 10, 2003, (Discussing the Egyptian TV miniseries *Horseman Without a Horse*, which dramatized content from *The Protocols of the Elders of Zion*).

84 "History of the Modern and Contemporary World," *Palestinian Authority Ministry of Education*, Grade 10 (2004): 60–61.

85 Berlet, C. and Lyons, M. N., *Right-wing populism in America: Too close for comfort* (Guilford Press, 2000). (This book discusses how far-right groups propagate antisemitic conspiracy theories, including the *Protocols*, to promote ideas like "Zionist Occupied Government.")

86 Snyder, T., *On tyranny: Twenty lessons from the twentieth century* (Tim Duggan Books, 2017). (Snyder explores how conspiracy theories, including those inspired by the *Protocols*, are sometimes used by extremist left-wing groups to demonize Israel and Jewish influence.)

87 The Covenant of the Islamic Resistance Movement [Hamas Charter]. (1988, August 18). Article 32. In *The Covenant of the Islamic Resistance Movement*. Avalon Project, Yale Law School. (States that "their plan is embodied in the 'Protocols of the Elders of Zion'…"

88 Political cartoon depicting Israeli Prime Minister Benjamin Netanyahu as a guide dog for U.S. President Donald Trump, *New York Times*, April 25, 2019, https://www.timesofisrael.com/international-new-york-times-to-cease-political-cartoons-after-anti-semitism-row/.

[89] Wilcox, C., "Editorial cartoon referencing Benjamin Netanyahu and calls for a royal commission," *The Sydney Morning Herald/The Age*, January 7, 2026.

[90] Findley, P., "They dare to speak out: People and institutions confront Israel's lobby," *Lawrence Hill & Company,* 1985.

[91] Specifically these accusations were made against the Israeli army on May 23, 2025, when an Israeli airstrike hit a home in Khan Yunis, Gaza, resulting in the deaths of nine of pediatrician Dr. Alaa al-Najjar's ten children and on July 10, 2025, when an Israeli airstrike in Deir al-Balah, central Gaza, killed at least 17 people, including many children and women who were waiting for nutritional supplements outside a Project HOPE clinic.

[92] "GenZ Now: Understanding and connecting with Jewish teens today," *The Jewish Education Project*, 2023, https://educator.jewishedproject.org/content/genz-now-jewish-teens-research-study.

[93] Windmueller, S., "In the wake of October 7: Reflections on the American Jewish community," *Jerusalem Center for Security and Foreign Affairs*, May 20, 2024, https://jcfa.org/in-the-wake-of-october-7-reflections-on-the-american-jewish-community/.

Chapter Six

[94] Troy, G. and Sharansky, N., "The unJews: The Jewish attempt to cancel Israel and Jewish peoplehood," *Tablet Magazine,* June 15, 2021, https://www.tabletmag.com/sections/news/articles/the-un-jews-natan-sharansky.

[95] The Altalena was a ship carrying weapons and fighters for the Irgun in 1948 that was sunk by the newly formed Israeli army on orders from David Ben-Gurion, highlighting the early Israeli state's insistence on a unified military and preventing independent militias.

[96] *2024 Survey of American Jewish Opinion* (American Jewish Committee, 2024).

[97] One example is Klein, E., "Why American Jews no longer understand one another," *New York Times*, July 20, 2025, https://www.nytimes.com/2025/07/20/opinion/antisemitism-american-jews-israel-mamdani.html.

98 Eilberg-Schwartz, P. and Eilberg, A., *The Distance We Have to Travel: Snapshot of an Intergenerational Jewish Conversation after October 7th* (Ayin Press, April 15, 2025), https://ayinpress.org/the-distance-we-have-to-travel/. For further context about this relationship, I would also recommend listening to the Judaism Unbound podcast featuring the mother and daughter Rabbi Amy Eilberg, and Penina Eilberg-Schwartz at Libenson, D., and Rofeberg, L., hosts, *Judaism Unbound Podcast,* "Israel-Palestine—Conversations across generations," August 7, 2025, https://www.youtube.com/watch?v=mdeZZ2G8JUo.

99 Eilberg, A., *The distance we have to travel: Snapshot of an intergenerational Jewish conversation on race* (Ayin Press November 15, 2023), https://ayinpress.org/the-distance-we-have-to-travel/.

100 *The Sefaria Midrash Rabbah*, trans. Joshua Schreier, 2022, *sefaria.org*, https://www.sefaria.org/Bereshit_Rabbah.48.9?lang=bi&with=all &lang2=en.

101 Fraiman, K. E., "Barriers to entry: Exploring educator reticence for engaging with the Israeli–Palestinian conflict," in S. Zakai and M. Reingold, eds., *Teaching Israel: Studies of pedagogy from the field* (Brandeis University Press, 2023), 229–254.

102 Fraiman, K. E., "The real barrier to Israel education isn't the conflict. It's us," *eJewish Philanthropy*, August 6, 2025, https://ejewishphilanthropy.com/the-real-barrier-to-israel-education-isnt-the-conflict-its-us/.

103 Burley, S., "U.S. Jewish institutions are purging their staffs of antiZionists," *In These Times*, October 1, 2024, https://inthesetimes.com/article/anti-zionist-israel-gaza-jewish-institutions.

104 Eisen, L., "Reimagining Israel education: 6 recommendations for catalyzing a new era," *eJewish Philanthropy*, June 9, 2025, https://ejewishphilanthropy.com/reimagining-israel-education-6-recommendations-for-catalyzing-a-new-era/?utm_source=chatgpt.com.

105 *Hadracha* is the Hebrew term for leadership, often referring to youth leadership training in Jewish educational and informal settings.

[106] Grimes, C., "A matter of interpretation: Examining the coded meanings of "safe space" in higher education communities," *Journal of Higher Education*, 90, no. 4, (2019): 547–567.

[107] Hooks, B., *Teaching to transgress: Education as the practice of freedom* (Routledge, 1994).

[108] Fish, R., "Navigating Complexity," *Dr. Rachel Fish* Blog, May 14, 2021. https://rachelfish.com/navigating-complexity/.

[109] Arao, B. and Clemens, K., "From safe spaces to brave spaces: A new way to frame dialogue around diversity and social justice," in *The art of effective facilitation: Reflections from social justice educators*, ed., L. Landreman (Sterling, VA: Stylus Publishing, 2013), 135–150.

[110] Reimer, J. and Bryfman, D., "What we know about experiential Jewish education," in *What we now know about Jewish education*, eds., R. Goodman, P. Flexner, and L. Bloomberg (Torah Aura Productions, 2008).

[111] Csikszentmihalyi, M., *Flow: The psychology of optimal experience* (Harper & Row, 1990).

[112] Reimer, J., "Beyond more Jews doing Jewish: Clarifying the goals of informal Jewish education," *Journal of Jewish Education* 73, no. 2 (2007): 5–19.

[113] *The Babylonian Talmud*, trans. Michael L. Rodkinson, Vol. III (New Talmud Publishing Society, 1916), 27–28, https://jewishvirtuallibrary.org/jsource/Judaism/FullTalmud.pdf.

[114] *Pirke Avot: The Sayings of the Jewish Fathers*, trans. Joseph I. Gorfinkle (Project Gutenberg, 1913) https://www.gutenberg.org/cache/epub/8547/pg8547-images.html.

[115] Backenroth, O. and Sinclair, A., "Reveling and unraveling in the face of Israel's complexity," *eJewishPhilanthropy*, August 2, 2013, https://ejewishphilanthropy.com/reveling-and-unraveling-in-the-face-of-israels-complexity.

[116] Zakai, S., *My second-favorite country: How American Jewish children think about Israel* (New York University Press, 2022).

[117] Between 1948 and the early 1950s, thousands of Yemenite children in Israel went missing from hospitals and immigrant camps, sparking allegations that they were forcibly taken from their families and

adopted without consent—a wound that remains a lasting symbol of injustice toward Mizrahi Jews.

118 In the early 1990s, many Ethiopian Jews immigrating to Israel were disproportionately infected with HIV through contaminated blood transfusions, exposing systemic negligence and racism in the healthcare system.

119 "Purity of Arms" (in Hebrew: טוהר הנשק, *Tohar HaNeshek*) is a foundational ethical principle of the Israel Defense Forces (IDF), part of its official Code of Ethics. It refers to the moral obligation of Israeli soldiers to use their weapons only for legitimate defense purposes and to maintain their humanity even during warfare.

Section Three

120 Kook, A. I., "Orot," *Sefaria,* https://www.sefaria.org/Orot.

121 Korczak, J., *The child's right to respect,* trans. E. E. Pilsudski (Human Development Poland, 1929/1999).

Chapter Seven

122 Translation by the author.

123 For the Sake of Argument is an Israelbased, nonpartisan educational initiative launched in 2022 by Abi Dauber Sterne and Robbie Gringras. It partners with Jewish communities to teach a structured "pedagogy of healthy argument," using stories, workshops, and training—initially focused on Israelrelated dialogue—to help participants engage in respectful disagreement, deepen understanding, and bridge community divides.

124 Klein, E., "Why American Jews no longer understand one another," *New York Times,* July 20, 2025, https://www.nytimes.com/2025/07/20/opinion/antisemitism-american-jews-israel-mamdani.html.

125 Itamar Ben-Gvir is an Israeli lawyer and far-right politician who has served as Israel's Minister of National Security since 2022. He leads the Otzma Yehudit (Jewish Power) party.

126 Bezalel Smotrich is an Israeli right-wing politician, leader of the Religious Zionism party, and currently serves as Israel's finance minister.

127 Efron, N., "These 3 progressive U.S. rabbis are the voices I trust right now," *The Times of Israel*, October 14, 2023, https://blogs.timesofisrael.com/these-3-progressive-us-rabbis-are-the-voices-i-trust-right-now/?utm_source=chatgpt.com.

128 This phrase comes from the Talmud, specifically Shavuot 39a. It expresses the foundational Jewish idea that all Jews are mutually bound spiritually, ethically, and communally.

129 The phrase *or l'goyim* originates in the Book of Isaiah, in which the prophet describes the role of Israel as a moral and spiritual example to the world: *"I, the Lord, have called you for a righteous purpose.... I will make you a covenant for the people and a light to the nations"* (Isaiah 42:6).

130 Ariel, J., "Becoming a cosmopolitan patriot: A perpetual imagining of Israel education," *Journal of Jewish Education* 89, no.3 (2023): 245–262.

131 Translation by the author.

132 According to Gaza War Hostage Crisis data, of 251 hostages, 44 percent had *only Israeli citizenship*, 37 percent held *dual nationality*, 19 percent were foreign nationals, and of the Israeli hostages six were Bedouins.

133 Bryfman, D., "Redeeming the hostages is the Jewish educational imperative of our lifetime," *eJewishPhilanthropy*, January 9, 2025, https://ejewishphilanthropy.com/redeeming-the-hostages-is-the-jewish-educational-imperative-of-our-lifetime/.

134 Forward Staff., "Watch: How Israeli-American hostage family Jon Polin and Rachel Goldberg-Polin brought the DNC to tears," *The Forward*, August 21, 2024, https://forward.com/fast-forward/646713/rachel-goldberg-polin-dnc-transcript-hostage-gaza-israel/.

135 "In every generation: A Haggadah supplement for 5784," *Hartman Institute,* April 5, 2024, https://www.hartman.org.il/wp-content/uploads/2024/04/In-Every-Generation-Seder-Supplement_FINAL_4.5.2024.pdf.

136 Ariel, J., "Becoming a cosmopolitan patriot: A perpetual imagining of Israel education," *Journal of Jewish Education* 89, no. 3, (2023): 245–262.

137 In the Talmud tractate Gittin 61a, the sages discuss situations of life and death, emphasizing that you cannot endanger yourself to save another based on the principle, "If you have bread in your basket, do not tell your neighbor to go hungry."

138 Seligman, M. E. P., *Flourish: A visionary new understanding of happiness and well-being* (Free Press, 2011).

Chapter Eight

139 The Machon L'Madrichei Chutz La'Aretz (מכון למדריכי חוץ לארץ), or Institute for Youth Leaders from Abroad, is a long-standing Zionist leadership training program in Israel. It is one of the most significant and historic programs for young Diaspora Jews, particularly those affiliated with Zionist youth movements.

140 A "Garin Nahal" (גרעין נח"ל), which refers to a group of young Israelis—often ideologically motivated—who combine military service with communal or social service, often in the form of a pioneering or Zionist project. (Nahal (נח"ל) is an acronym for Noar Halutzi Lohem (נוער חלוצי לוחם), meaning "Fighting Pioneer Youth.")

141 Cohen, S. M. and Kelman, A. Y., "Beyond distancing: Young adult American Jews and their alienation from Israel," *The Andrea and Charles Bronfman Philanthropies,* 2007; and "A portrait of Jewish Americans: Findings from a Pew Research Center survey of U.S. Jews," *Pew Research Center*, 2013, https://www.pewresearch.org/religion/2013/10/01/jewish-american-beliefs-attitudes-culture-survey/.

142 Sasson, T., Kadushin, C., and Saxe, L., *American Jewish attachment to Israel: An assessment of the 'distancing' hypothesis* (Brandeis University 2007).

143 Ezer Weizman (June 15, 1924–April 24, 2005) was an Israeli major general and politician who served as the president of Israel, first elected in 1993 and re-elected in 1998. Before the presidency, Weizman was commander of the Israeli Air Force and Minister of Defense.

144 Herzog's *Voice of the People* initiative is a global listening project launched by Israeli President Isaac Herzog after October 7 to engage

Jews worldwide in shaping a shared Jewish future through dialogue and reflection.

145 Herzl, T., *The Jewish State*, trans. D. Littman (Dover Publications, 1988).

146 "Jewish Americans in 2020," *Pew Research Center,* May 11, 2021, https://www.pewresearch.org/religion/2021/05/11/jewish-identity-and-belief/.

147 "U.S. Jews' political views," *Pew Research Center,* May 11, 2021, https://www.pewresearch.org/religion/2021/05/11/u-s-jews-political-views/.

148 "Jewish Americans in 2020," *Pew Research Center,* May 11, 2021, https://www.pewresearch.org/religion/2021/05/11/jewish-identity-and-belief/.

149 "Jewish Americans in 2020," *Pew Research Center,* May 11, 2021, https://www.pewresearch.org/religion/2021/05/11/jewish-identity-and-belief/.

150 Margalit, A., *The Ethics of Memory* (Harvard University Press, 2004).

151 Ravid, S., "Jewish Peoplehood: What does it mean and why is it important?," *Journal of Jewish Communal Service* 83, no. 1 (2008): 6–11.

152 The phrase is most famously connected to Rashi's commentary on Exodus 19:2, describing the Israelites encamped at Mount Sinai right before receiving the Torah: *"Vayichan sham Yisrael neged hahar"*— "And Israel encamped there opposite the mountain." Rashi notes that the Hebrew verb for "encamped" (וַיִּחַן) is singular, even though it refers to all the Israelites. He explains: "כְּאִישׁ אֶחָד בְּלֵב אֶחָד"— *"Like one person with one heart."*

153 Enter: The Jewish Peoplehood Alliance is a global initiative dedicated to strengthening Jewish identity, connection, and collective responsibility across diverse communities worldwide.

154 These include programs such as Diller Teen Fellows and The Bronfman Youth Fellowships in Israel (BYFI), and Hevruta Gap-Year Program offered by the Shalom Hartman Institute.

[155] Ladon, J. and Sagiv, M., *Israel at war – Being the Jews we want to be* (Shalom Hartman Institute, October 19 2023), https://www.hartman.org.il/being-the-jews-we-want-to-be/.

[156] Rose, D., "The world of the Jewish youth movement," in *The Encyclopedia of Pedagogy and Informal Education* (2005), https://infed.org/dir/welcome/the-world-of-the-jewish-youth-movement/.

[157] Z3 (short for Zionism 3.0) is a vision and initiative created by Zack Bodner and the Oshman Family JCC in Palo Alto.

[158] Bodner, Z., "Reclaiming the Z-word" in *SAPIR: A Journal of Jewish Conversations*, Volume Five (May 6, 2022).

[159] "The distancing from Israel hypothesis is disturbingly re-affirmed," *American Enterprise Institute*, March 6, 2024, https://www.aei.org/op-eds/the-distancing-from-israel-hypothesis-is-disturbingly-re-affirmed/.

[160] Ze'ev Jabotinsky (1880–1940) was a Zionist leader, orator, and founder of Revisionist Zionism, advocating for a Jewish state on both sides of the Jordan River and for a strong Jewish self-defense.

[161] Rav Abraham Isaac Kook (1865–1935), the first Ashkenazi Chief Rabbi of Mandatory Palestine, was a pioneering Jewish mystic and thinker who saw secular Zionism as part of a divine process of redemption and sought to unify religious and secular Jews.

[162] Menachem Begin (1913–1992) was the leader of Israel's Irgun underground, founder of the Likud party, and sixth Prime Minister of Israel, best known for signing the 1979 peace treaty with Egypt.

[163] Ber Borochov (1881–1917) was a Marxist Zionist theorist who argued that a Jewish national homeland and a socialist society were mutually necessary for the economic and social revival of the Jewish people.

[164] A.D. Gordon (1856–1922) was a Zionist thinker who championed *Labor Zionism*, emphasizing the spiritual and national rejuvenation of Jews through manual labor and a close connection to the land of Israel.

[165] Berl Katznelson (1887–1944) was a leading Labor Zionist thinker and journalist who helped shape the ideological and social

foundations of the Yishuv and the Histadrut, promoting Jewish labor, socialism, and communal settlement in Palestine.

166 Troy, G., *The Zionist ideas: Visions for the Jewish homeland—Then, now, tomorrow* (Jewish Publication Society, 2018).

167 Stowe-Lindner, J., "Teaching Zionism in an age of moral complexity," *The Jewish Independent*, August 7, 2025, https://thejewishindependent.com.au/teaching-zionism-in-an-age-of-moral-complexity.

168 Breakstone, D., "Not my Jewish state," *The Times of Israel*, August 29, 2022, https://blogs.timesofisrael.com/not-my-jewish-state/.

169 Brandeis, L. D., "The Jewish problem: How to solve it," P. R. Mendes-Flohr and J. Reinharz, eds., *The Jew in the modern world: A documentary history* (Oxford University Press, 1975), 556–561.

170 The Dreyfus Affair was a late-19th-century French political scandal in which Alfred Dreyfus, a Jewish army officer, was falsely convicted of treason, exposing the deep roots of antisemitism, nationalism, and injustice in modern Europe.

171 Amongst other contexts, this issue is raised in the memoir of Pennsylvania Governor Josh Shapiro, who described being interrogated about his connections to Israel when he was being vetted as a possible Democratic Party nominee for vice-president in the 2024 election. In the end, Shapiro was not nominated. Shapiro, J. D., *Where We Keep the Light: Stories from a Life of Service* (HarperCollins 2026).

172 Ahad Ha'Am (pen name of Asher Ginzberg, 1856–1927) was a leading Jewish thinker who advocated for *Cultural Zionism*, emphasizing the renewal of Jewish spiritual and cultural life over immediate political statehood.

173 Eliezer Ben-Yehuda (1858–1922) was a Jewish lexicographer and revivalist who led the effort to transform Hebrew into a modern spoken language and is often called the "father of modern Hebrew."

174 Shapero, J., "Grappling with Israel through its arts: Students explore Israeli arts to foster questioning and connection," *The Covenant Foundation*, 2024, https://covenantfn.org/articles/grappling-with-israel-

through-it-arts-students-explore-israeli-arts-to-foster-questioning-and-connection/.

175 Burley, S., "U.S. Jewish institutions are purging their staffs of anti-Zionists," *Europe Solidaire Sans Frontières*, October 1, 2024, https://www.europe-solidaire.org/spip.php?article72191.

176 *Shlichim* are emissaries or representatives sent by a Jewish organization, usually from Israel, and often from The Jewish agency for Israel, to communities abroad to strengthen Jewish identity, education, and Israel-Diaspora connections.

177 *Shinshinim* are recent Israeli high school graduates who spend a year volunteering abroad before their military service, typically through programs run by The Jewish Agency for Israel.

Chapter Nine

178 Important to note that the full text of the resolutions clearly also calls for two states to be established in the area known as Israel and for Israel to withdraw from occupied territories.

179 From a speech given by Martin Luther King Jr. on March 25, 1968, at appearance at the Rabbinical Assembly, just 10 days before his assassination.

180 Weissman, N., "Celebration and exploration: Why good Israel education needs both," *Unpacked Education,* April 12, 2023, https://unpacked.education/blog/celebration-and-exploration-why-good-israel-education-needs-both.

181 AIPAC is the American Israel Public Affairs Committee, a lobbying group in the United States that advocates for strong United States–Israel relations.

182 Twenge, J. M., *Generations: The real differences between Gen Z, Millennials, Gen X, Boomers, and Silents—and what they mean for America's future* (Atria Books 2023).

183 *Should Jews criticize other Jews in public?* (Shalom Hartman Institute February 5, 2023), https://www.hartman.org.il/should-jews-criticize-other-jews-in-public-transcript/.

184 "Dua Lipa denounces 'Israeli genocide' in Instagram post," *The Guardian*, May 29, 2024, https://www.theguardian.com/music/

article/2024/may/29/dua-lipa-denounces-israeli-genocide-in-instagram-post.

[185] *Declaration of the establishment of the State of Israel,* Provisional Council of State of Israel, Government of Israel, May 14, 1948.

Chapter Ten

[186] Israeli Arabs (also referred to as Arab citizens of Israel) are Palestinian Arabs who remained within the borders of the State of Israel after its establishment in 1948 and hold Israeli citizenship.

[187] Nierenberg, A., "Israeli forces rescue Bedouin hostage held by Hamas in Gaza," *New York Times,* August 27, 2024, https://www.nytimes.com/2024/08/27/world/middleeast/israel-gaza-hostage-bedouin.html. For fuller account of incident Partners in Fate, posted in 2023, https://www.youtube.com/watch?v=CrXtTYm_NB8.

[188] Dinero, S. C., "Image is everything: The development of the Negev Bedouin as a tourist attraction," *Nomadic Peoples* 6, no.1, (2022): 69–94.

[189] Rosenthal, D., *The Israelis: Ordinary people in an extraordinary land* (Free Press 2008).

[190] Myers, M. and Roth, A., "The struggle for Bedouin land rights and identity in modern Israel," *The Jerusalem Post,* August 21, 2024, https://www.jpost.com/israel-news/article-815691.

[191] "Israel's Nation-State Law: A comprehensive overview," *Israel Democracy Institute,* July 31, 2019, https://en.idi.org.il/articles/24241.

[192] Kitchens, B., Johnson, S. L., and Gray, P., "Understanding Echo Chambers and Filter Bubbles: The Impact of Social Media on Diversification and Partisan Shifts in News Consumption," *Journal of Strategic Information Systems,* 2020. Del Vicario, M., Vivaldo, G., Bessi, A., Zollo, F., Scala, A., Caldarelli, G., and Quattrociocchi, W., "Echo Chambers: Emotional Contagion and Group Polarization on Facebook," *National Library of Medicine, Scientific Reports* 6, no. 37825 (2016), https://pmc.ncbi.nlm.nih.gov/articles/PMC5131349/.

[193] Buber, M., *I and Thou,* trans. W. Kaufmann (Charles Scribner's Sons, 1970), 11.

194 Noddings, N., *The challenge to care in schools: An alternative approach to education* 2 (Teachers College Press, 2005).

195 Graham-Harrison, E. and Kierszenbaum, Q., "Israeli police raid Jerusalem bookshops and arrest Palestinian owners," *The Guardian,* February 10, 2025.

196 The term "hilltop youth" refers to a loosely organized group of young Israeli settlers, primarily religious-nationalist teens and young adults, who live on or establish unauthorized settlements (often called *outposts*) in the West Bank, usually on hilltops.

197 Bryfman, D, host, *Adapting: The Future of Jewish Education,* "Israel education in a post-October 7th world: What does it mean to bear witness?, " The Jewish Education Project, March 28, 2024, https://podcasts.apple.com/us/podcast/israel-education-in-a-post-october-7th-world-what/id1541392566?i=1000650711231.

198 Bryfman, D., "All education is political. Jewish education should be, too." *The Forward,* October 6, 2020. Based largely on Foucault, M., *The archaeology of knowledge & the discourse on language,* trans. A. M. Sheridan Smith (Pantheon Books 1972/1977).

199 Khalidi, R., *The Hundred Years' War on Palestine: A history of settler colonialism and resistance, 1917–2017* (Metropolitan Books, 2020), 45.

200 The phrase, *"A land without a people for a people without a land"* is often linked to the Zionist movement but has a complex history. Originally used in 1843 by a Christian Restorationist clergyman, it was widely employed by Christian Restorationists for nearly a century. Its use among Jewish Zionists is debated: some scholars argue it was never common, while others, like Anita Shapira, contend it was widely used around the turn of the 20th century. Israel Zangwill, a prominent Zionist-turned-critic, notably used the phrase in 1901, describing Palestine as "a country without a people" and Jews as "a people without a country."

201 The phrase "The Arabs never miss an opportunity to miss an opportunity" is most commonly attributed to Abba Eban, who was Israel's diplomat and later Foreign Minister, in Eban, A., *Abba Eban: An autobiography* (Random House, 1977).

202 Campbell, J., *The Power of Myth with Bill Moyers* (Anchor Books, 1988).

203 Isaacs, A., "Israel education: Purposes and practices," in *HaYidion: The Prizmah Journal of Jewish Education* (Springer, Dordrecht, 2009), 22–25.

204 The Law of Return is an Israeli law, passed in 1950 and amended several times since, that grants every Jew the right to immigrate to Israel and obtain Israeli citizenship.

205 The Status Quo Agreement refers to an informal arrangement made in 1947–1948 between David Ben-Gurion, Israel's first Prime Minister, and the ultra-Orthodox (Haredi) Jewish leadership regarding the role of religion in the newly established State of Israel.

206 The Nation-State Law (officially, the Basic Law: Israel as the Nation-State of the Jewish People) is an Israeli law passed in 2018 that defines Israel explicitly as the nation-state of the Jewish people.

207 This scenario was adapted from Gradstein, L., Halpern, G., and Efron, N., hosts, *The Promised Podcast*, season 15, episode 1, "Gaza: Yesterday & Tomorrow," TLV1 Studios, August 6, 2025, https://traffic.libsyn.com/promised/TPP_6-8-25.mp3.

208 Ecclesiastes 1:9, *Tanakh: The Holy Scriptures* (JPS, 1985).

209 One such example is, "Younger Americans stand out in their views of the IsraelHamas war, showing more sympathy for Palestinians relative to older adults," *Pew Research Center,* 2024, https://www.pewresearch.org/short-reads/2024/04/02/younger-americans-stand-out-in-their-views-of-the-israel-hamas-war/.

210 "Lone soldiers reflect on reason for making aliyah, join war effort," *Ynetnews*, November 21, 2024, https://www.ynetnews.com/article/hyuktdnmjg.

211 Heilman, Y., "Diary of an IDF Soldier," *Sapir Journal* (October 2023–February 2024): Parts I–X, https://sapirjournal.org/war-in-israel/2023/dispatches-from-a-soldier/.

212 *The Babylonian Talmud*, vol. VI, trans. Michael L. Rodkinson (New Talmud Publishing Society, 1916), 10, https://jewishvirtuallibrary.org/jsource/Judaism/FullTalmud.pdf.

Chapter Eleven

[213] *The Holy Scriptures: A New Translation* (Jewish Publication Society, 1917).

[214] Susanna Lachs Adler., "More Joy, Less Oy: Remarks from the Main Event," *Jewish Federation of Greater Philadelphia*, November 14, 2019, https://blog.jewishphilly.org/more-joy-less-oy-remarks-from-the-main-event.

[215] "Campus Antisemitism Report Card™," *AntiDefamation League*, 2025, https://www.adl.org/es/node/76351.

[216] B. Berger, *personal communications*, August 14, 2025.

[217] RootOne is a North American initiative designed to provide Jewish teens with immersive summer experiences in Israel. Launched by The Jewish Education Project and seeded by a generous gift from The Marcus Foundation, RootOne aims to strengthen Jewish identity and foster a deeper connection to Israel among Jewish teens.

[218] Chazan, B., *The Philosophy of Informal Jewish Education* (The Jewish Agency for Israel, 2002).

[219] Cohen, S. M. and Eisen, A., *The Jew within: Self, identity, and belonging in contemporary Jewish life* (Indiana University Press, 2000).

Horowitz, B., "Connections and journeys: Shifting identities among American Jews," *Jewish Continuity Commission* (1998).

[220] Sacks, J., "The hatred that won't die," *The Guardian*, February 28, 2002, https://www.theguardian.com/world/2002/feb/28/comment.

[221] Lobell, K. O., "A Free Man Instilling Pride in Jews," *Jewish Journal*, April 14, 2023, https://jewishjournal.com/community/357859/afreemaninstillingprideinjews. Further expanded in his book, Freeman, B. M., *Jewish Pride: Rebuilding a People* (Whitefox Publishing, 2021).

[222] Rachel Fish from Boundless is one such example who has written and spoken extensively about greater knowledge leading to more Jewish pride.

Fish, R., "Israel literacy: Cultivating literacy and critical thinking about Israel within Jewish and Israel education," *Journal of Jewish Education* 89, no. 1, (2023): 4–25.

[223] "The Jewish Education Project," *Jewish Pride Outcomes,* 2024, https://educator.jewishedproject.org/sites/default/files/2024-11/Jewish%20Pride%20Outcomes.pdf.

[224] Chazan, B., *A philosophy of Israel education: A relational approach* (Springer 2019).

[225] Israel, S., "Teaching Israel, teaching truth: A personal view from the front." *The Lookstein Center*, 2008, https://www.lookstein.org/journal/fall-2008/teaching-israel-teaching-truth-personal-view-front/.

[226] Gringras, R., *Hugging and wrestling: Alternative paradigm for the Diaspora–Israel relationship* (The Jewish Agency for Israel, Makom: Renewing Israel Engagement, 2006).

[227] Winer, L. N. (2019). "Teaching who they are: American-born supplementary school teachers' connections with Israel," (Doctoral diss., The Jewish Theological Seminary, 2019).

[228] Bitton, M., " *SAPIR Journal,* November 1, 2023, https://sapirjournal.org/war-in-israel/2023/that-pain-youre-feeling-is-peoplehood/.

[229] Bitton, M., "*Committed by Mijal Bitton,* October 17, 2023, https://mijal.substack.com/p/bereshit-the-joy-we-are-feeling-is.

Conclusion

[230] Theory U is a change management framework by Otto Scharmer that guides individuals and organizations to shift from reacting to problems toward creating the future by moving through a process of *co-initiating, co-sensing, presencing, co-creating, and co-evolving.*

[231] Scharmer, C. O., *Theory U: Leading from the emerging future* (Berrett-Koehler, 2007).

[232] Ofakim is a small development town in Israel's Negev Desert, founded in 1955, known for its working-class community, textile industry origins, and resilience during conflicts.

[233] On October 7, 2023, Hamas gunmen entered the city of Ofakim, where residents endured hours of fighting and hostage situations inside their homes. Local civilians, alongside police and security forces, fought back, and Ofakim became one of the southern Israeli towns symbolizing both the horror and heroism of that day.

[234] Dewey, J., *The quest for certainty: A study of the relation of knowledge and action* (Minton, Balch & Company, 1929), 178.

[235] Sacks, J., *Future tense: Jews, Judaism, and Israel in the twenty-first century* (Schocken, 2009), 233.

[236] Anemone tubers can be bought in the United States, and are referred to as wind flowers. A story about Kalaniyot, https://www.riverdalepress.com/stories/the-fascinating-flower-story-of-a-poppy-and-a-kalaniyot,68230.

[237] One of the members of our delegation is a mother of a woman who survived the Nova festival.

[238] "הַמִּלְחָמָה הָאַחֲרוֹנָה" (*Hamilchama Ha'achrona*), "The Last War," performed by Yehoram Gaon during the 1973 Yom Kippur War. The lyrics were written by Chaim Hefer and composed by Dubi (Dov) Seltzer, and Gaon performed it live for troops on the front lines during that tense period.

Epilogue

[239] Koplow, M., "Israel Policy Forum's Michael Koplow: Hostage deal 'frees up' U.S. Jewry for long-term initiatives," interview by Dayanim, N., *eJewishPhilanthropy*, October 10, 2025, https://ejewishphilanthropy.com/israel-policy-forums-michael-koplow-hostage-deal-frees-up-u-s-jewry-for-long-term-initiatives/?utm_source=cio.

[240] Creditor, M., "A Prayer for Burying 'Bring Them Home Now' Dog Tags," *The Times of Israel*, October 10, 2025.

[241] Bring Home Now (@BringHomeNow), "Our struggle is not over. It will not end until the last hostage is located and returned for proper burial," Twitter (now X), October 13, 2025, https://x.com/bringhomenow/status/1977621313993814360.

[242] Horowitz, B., "Connections and Journeys: Assessing Critical Opportunities for Enhancing Jewish Identity," *UJAFederation of Jewish Philanthropies of New York*, 2003.

ACKNOWLEDGMENTS

Within hours of October 7, I knew that this moment was different. Instinctively, I reached out to a small circle of trusted colleagues. What began as urgent phone calls quickly became an ongoing lifeline. Over the months that followed, we wrote together, spoke together, argued together, and brought hundreds of educators to Israel. Yet the most important work we did was quieter: showing up for one another.

These colleagues did not remain just collaborators for long. They became the support network that carried me through some of the most disorienting and challenging moments of my professional and personal life.

I cannot fully imagine what these past two years would have looked like without Abi, Alana, Anne, Assaf, Ayala, Ben and Ben, Clare, Dan, Freda, Hana, Howie, Ilan, Jeremy, Jonny, Keren, Liz, Marcie, Maya, Noam, Osnat, Paul, Rachel, Robbie, Scot, Shai, Shelley, Shuki, Yoni, Zohar, and many others whom I regrettably cannot name here. It would have been lonelier, and it would have been poorer in spirit.

I owe a particular debt to my Israeli colleagues and friends—those named above and many more on the ground—who introduced me to the lived reality of a post-October 7 world. You trusted me with expressions of your shock, pain, anger, and exhaustion, as well as, at times, your unexpected laughter. You understood my guilt at not always being physically alongside you and you still held me close. I will always carry that generosity of spirit with me.

Many people shaped my journey as an Israel educator long before I had language for what that even meant. Steve Israel, Chaim Feder, Roy Graham, and Laura Janner-Klausner planted early seeds, likely without realizing they were doing so. I owe much to Howie Deitcher for making Jewish texts feel open and alive, Jeffrey Lasday for taking a risk on an unknown Australian, Robert Sherman for weaving supervision with mentorship, and to Jonathan Woocher of blessed memory, whose understanding of the power of ideas in education remains unmatched.

Along my journey I have been supported by the Jewish community itself, benefiting directly as a Wexner Graduate Fellow; a Schusterman Fellow, Preside; and being part Leading Edge's CEO Onboarding program. All of this contributed to my understanding of the American Jewish landscape, my deep commitment to pluralism, and a core belief that as a Jewish community we are all in this together.

No one has influenced my work in Israel education more than Barry Chazan, who appeared repeatedly at formative junctures, introduced me to Yehuda Amichai and John Dewey (and everyone in between), and challenged me with generosity and insistence. I remain deeply indebted to him.

I am grateful to Karen Everett, president of The Jewish Education Project, and to the recent leadership of Lois Kohn-Claar, Martine Fleishman, and the entire board of the organization for granting me a sabbatical in the summer of 2025. That time was both restorative and essential. It gave me the space to breathe, reflect, and begin making sense of events that resisted easy framing. This book would not exist without that hiatus.

I also thank the professional staff of the agency, and especially the leadership team—Susan Wachsstock, Steve Goldberg, Nessa Liben, Amy Amiel, Dena Klein, and Simon Amiel—for making that time possible and for the daily privilege of working alongside them, as well as enormous gratitude to Dina Nusnbaum for assisting to actualize this book, as well as every other project I embark upon.

Over the past year and a half, I have been fortunate enough to partner with a group of individuals deeply committed to reimagining Israel education. I thank Dawne Bear Novicoff, Aviva Jacobs, Rella Kaplowitz, Seffi Kogen, and Anna Langer of who all exemplify not only professional excellence, but also what partnership can look like at its best: thoughtful, values-driven, and grounded in trust.

I feel privileged to have been in an ongoing *chevruta* with Beth Cousens and Dena Klein, involved in an intellectual and moral partnership that sharpened my thinking and sustained this project at critical moments.

I thank David Hazony of the Z3 Institute for taking on this book, Rabbi Amitai Fraiman for recognizing the vision behind it, Zack Bodner for his steadfast leadership, and Benjamin Kerstein for editing the manuscript with such care, intelligence, and quiet wisdom.

I am thankful to Jonny Ariel, Zack Bodner, Rachel Fish, Keren Fraiman, Ben Jacobs, Shelley Kedar, Rachel Jacoby Rosenfield, Miriam Heller Stern, Abi Dauber Sterne, and Noam Weissman who read sections of this manuscript and engaged with it seriously. They did so not out of obligation, but out of a shared commitment to the field of Israel and Jewish education. Their questions and pushback made this a better book. And enduring appreciation to Zohar Raviv, who also undertook the task of writing the foreword to this book with the same care and precision he brings to all of his educational work.

My mother, who has been gone for more than a decade, was the first great educator I ever knew, at home and in the classroom. My father was my first Zionist role model and alongside his unwavering support for me (and for the Collingwood Magpies), I will always remember the image of him standing shoulder-to-shoulder with David Ben-Gurion. With such an inheritance, this book feels less like an individual act and more like a continuation of a family story; one that my sister, Donna, carries forward every day as the finest educator of young people I know.

To my Brooklyn family, this acknowledgment is both an apology for my distraction and absences over the past few years and an expression of gratitude for your patience and support. Jonah and Abby, you encountered images and conversations that should never become familiar to children your age, and yet you met them with curiosity and empathy. You fill me with pride and confidence in the Jewish adults you are fast becoming. Mirm has been my constant, holding our world together, supporting my work, and standing beside me always. Except, of course, when we run. Then she leads from the front, as she did in our impulsive decision to run the Tel Aviv half-marathon in 2024, a morning of unexpected normalcy in Israel and one I will never forget.

Finally, I thank you, the readers of this book. If you have reached these pages, it is likely that you, too, have been on a journey since October 7. I see you. My hope is that this book can serve you, in some small way, as a companion as we move together through these days toward the better ones that must come.

ABOUT THE AUTHOR

Author Photo by Mitchell "Moshe" Schack

Dr. David Bryfman is the chief executive officer of The Jewish Education Project, a national leader in innovating Jewish education and supporting educators. As an internationally recognized speaker and writer, David offers expertise on Israel education, the trends of Jewish education today, and the innovations necessary to shape Jewish education tomorrow. David earned his doctorate from NYU in Education and Jewish Studies, and is an alum of the Wexner Graduate Fellowship and Schusterman Fellowship. David is also an Adjunct Fellow at The Z3 Institute and hosts the weekly podcast *Adapting: The Future of Jewish Education*, where he explores pressing topics with expert guests. David lives in Brooklyn, New York, with his wife Mirm, and two children, Jonah and Abby.

www.ingramcontent.com/pod-product-compliance
Lightning Source LLC
LaVergne TN
LVHW010607100826
845148LV00014B/2885